ADVANCED KENPO KARATE

Revised Edition

by Jay T. Will

EMPIRE BOOK/AWP LLC
Los Angeles, CA.

DISCLAIMER

Please note that the author and publisher of this book are NOT RESPONSIBLE in any manner whatsoever for any injury that may result from practicing the techniques and/or following the instructions given within. Since the physical activities described herein may be too strenuous in nature for some readers to engage in safely, it is essential that a physician be consulted prior to training.

Revised Edition published in 2019 by AWP LLC/Empire Books. Copyright (c) 2019 by Jay T. Will and AWP LLC/Empire Books.

All rights reserved. No part of this publication may be reproduced or utilized in any form or by any means, electronic or mechanical, including photo- copying, recording, or by any information storage and retrieval system, without prior written permission from AWP LLC/Empire Books.

Revised edition Library of Congress Catalog Number:

ISBN-13: 978-1-949753-77-6

19 18 17 16 15 14 13 12

Library of Congress Cataloging-in-Publication Data

Advanced Kenpo Karate by Jay T. Will -- ed. p. cm.

ISBN 978-1-949753-77-6 (pbk. : alk. paper) 1. Martial arts-- technique. 3. Large type books. I. Title. GV1114.3.F715 20711161.815'3--dc22

21981187543

Printed in the United States of America.

ADVANCED KENPO KARATE

Revised Edition

Dedication: This book is dedicated to Linda, whose support has always been appreciated.

Acknowledgement: I would like to express my sincere thanks to those who helped make this book possible. To Ed Parker, my first instructor who encouraged me to experiment; to Dave King and Ed Ikuta for their patience and expert knowledge of martial arts photography during the photo sessions for this book; to Steve Gerhardt who demonstrated with me during the photo sessions; to Mark Komuro and Alan Takemoto, two of the best art directors in the business; and to Curtis Wong, a friend who encouraged me and allowed me to make this book a reality.

INTRODUCTION

Cursing under his breath, a huge man clomps his way along the wharfside streets, and into the night. A young cocker spaniel streaks after him, playfully. Thud! The dog whelps loudly, whimpering into the darkness, away from the man's kick. The man curses once more. The world hates him. He pulls a bottle of whiskey from his coat pocket, and gulps it down. Then the man tenses, like an attack dog. He's spotted *you*.

"Hey, kid!" the big man bellows. His words make the cold night suddenly colder, "I don't like your face." The man lunges at you, his right hand cocking backward into a wild haymaker.

You are an advanced student of Kenpo. Instantly, you must decide on a defense. What do you do? Dance away and counterkick his punch? Not a bad plan . . . especially against a man of this size. Unfortunately, you are standing in a telephone booth. Now what do you do?

The Kenpo fighting system is based on the concept of flexibility. The fundamental techniques are designed to be flexible enough that they can be adapted to the physical limitations of the student. Further, the applications of those techniques are kept flexible enough that they can be adapted to any self-defense situation. In Kenpo, techniques are fitted to the individual just as a tailor fits a new suit to the customer.

Advanced Kenpo must be understood within the context of flexibility. Like the Kenpo system itself, the techniques within these covers are down-to-earth, practical, and functional. They are considered advanced because they require more dexterity and coordination between the hands, feet, knees and elbows. But, as always, they can be modified slightly to fit a new situation.

The techniques in *Advanced Kenpo* are constructed around Kenpo's principle of duplicity. Each technique contains several movements. The motive is simple. If the attacker is not disabled by the initial blow, the follow-up combinations should finish the job. On the street, Kenpo practitioners confront an attacker with the forethought of using all the movements of each technique. If the attacker is subdued early, so much the better.

Perhaps each basic Kenpo technique should be thought of as a "letter" in an alphabet of motion. *Advanced* techniques add letters to your alphabet. The more advanced letters you learn, the more letters you add to your alphabet of motion. You are then able to create "words" of motion by combining the letters. The more you progress, the larger your alphabetical motion will become, eventually enabling you to form "phrases." Finally, you will be able to create "sentences" from the words.

The techniques of *Advanced Kenpo* may not be used exactly as you see them in sequence. They give you an entire spectrum of "language" from which to choose. You may use a movement from one technique, another movement from a second technique, and yet another from a third to create what is workable for you in a given situation. This process is similar to choosing the best words to construct a good sentence. From this basis the aggregate execution of Kenpo's alphabet of motion becomes infinite.

Now, still another aspect of the alphabet of motion can be mentioned -- subtraction. The word "and" must be removed from the Kenpo vocabulary. When applying Kenpo techniques, then, each movement from the alphabet of motion will be combined with others *without* the word "and." For example: block, punch, elbow. Not block, *and* punch, *and* elbow.

By removing the concept of "and," you remove any hesitation in the execution of techniques. There will be no time-gap between any static motion and a static motion and a self-defense maneuver. The techniques will then *flow* smoothly as water poured from a glass.

The contents of *Advanced Kenpo,* if practiced earnestly, greatly expand a student's language of motion. They will give you more techniques to add to your existing pool of knowledge. Thus, these techniques will develop your ability to confront a variety of situations, to remain flexible.

When learning the Kenpo techniques, be aware of the "clock principle." The clock principle helps the student to visually imagine which direction he is to follow. He is asked to think of himself as being in the middle of a clock facing 12 o'clock, with six o'clock to the rear three and nine o'clock to his right and left respectively, and all other numbers in their respective places.

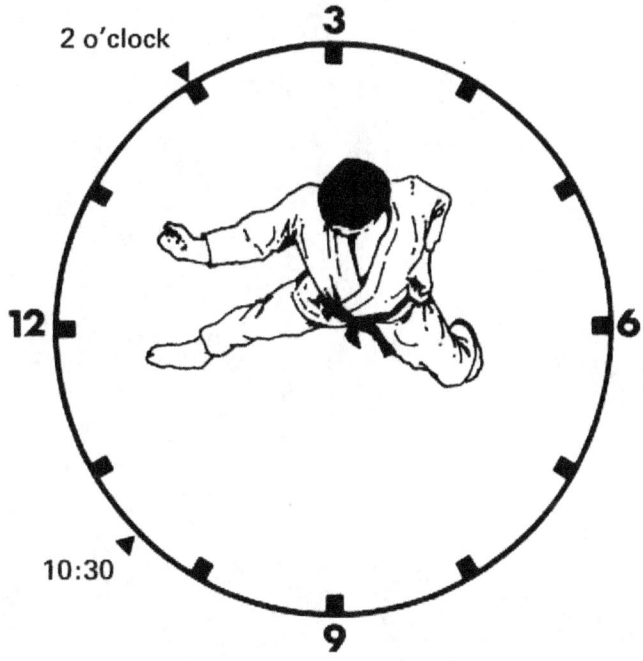

CONTENTS

	LOCKOUT PUNCH	10
	REVERSE PUNCH	12
	BACKFIST	14
1	KUNG-FU CROSS	16
2	DIVIDED SWORD	20
3	ARM HOOK	24
4	CROSSING THE SUN	28
5	OPENING THE FAN	32
6	WING BREAK	36
7	DARKNESS	40
8	FLASHING WINGS	44
9	SNAPPING TWIG	48
10	PLAYER OF DEATH	52
11	RISING KICK	56
12	CIRCLE OF CHINA	60
13	OPENING COWL	64
14	STICKS OF SATAN	68
15	DANCER	72
16	THE BRIDGE	76
17	ROCKING ELBOW	80
18	AIMING THE SPEAR	84
19	U-PUNCH	88
20	UNCOVERING THE FLAME	92
21	COVERING THE FLAME	96
22	DOUBLE BLADES	100
23	LEVELING THE CLOUDS	104
24	CIRCLES OF GLASS	108
25	FALLING HEEL	112
26	THE SICKLE	116
27	WATERFALL	120
	A LEAP OF FAITH	125
	A NO-NONSENSE APPROACH TO KENPO	130

LOCKOUT PUNCH
FROM TRAINING HORSE STANCE

FRONT VIEW

SIDE VIEW

Throwing the lockout punch from the training horse stance helps us develop the proper form, speed, power and technique so that we can apply it to the more practical and useful reverse punch. *TRAINING TIP* — It will be very helpful if you practice the lockout punch while standing in front of a mirror. Be sure to watch your elbows and make sure that the elbows do not come out when punching. The motion that is desired is the elbow should rub along your ribs as you throw the punch.

NOTE: Be sure to keep your head at the same level while punching, and remember to turn your shoulders into the punch.

REVERSE PUNCH
FROM THE FIGHTING HORSE STANCE

FRONT VIEW

SIDE VIEW

    The reverse punch is different from the lockout punch in that we are now standing in the type of stance that we will use in a realistic fighting or self defense situation. We are now in a stance that gives us maximum protection, and allows us maximum mobility at the same time. When throwing the reverse punch, you will want to turn your shoulder into the punch to give maximum range and penetration. We will also pull the punch back so that we can maintain control over our body. We do not want to overextend our body while punching, we must maintain control. If we do not have control over our *own* body, we cannot control our opponent.

    After we have graduated from the lockout punch from the training horse stance to the reverse punch from the side fighting stance, it is important *not* to go back to practicing the lockout punch. From this point on we will only practice the *REVERSE PUNCH* as it will be used in a

NOTE: Be sure to keep your head at the same level while punching, and remember to turn your shoulders into the punch.

realistic, practical self defense situation. *TRAINING TIP* — Again, it is very important to keep our elbow in close to our body while punching. This can be helped along when practicing, standing next to a wall with your shoulder approximately 6 to 8 inches away from the wall. This exercise will be of great value in keeping your elbow in close to your body while punching, because if your elbow moves out away from the body, the elbow will make contact with the wall. If you are able to punch consistently without making elbow contact on the wall, you will have a reverse punch that does not telegraph.

Even the worst fighter reacts to movements, and since the elbow movement tells him something is on the way, we can virtually remove all advanced warning.

BACKFIST

FRONT-QUARTER VIEW

NOTE: You must relax your wrist in order to attain a fast whipping motion.

The Backfist Strike

The backfist strike is the karatekas jab. The difference is, however, that the backfist can do much more damage, making it very practical. This technique also gives us maximum range and maximum protection since we do not have to compromise our body position in order to use it effectively. If the backfist is used properly, it is virtually unstoppable.

The three secrets to a fast effective backfist are: First, most instructors are very *FORM* conscious, hence they will have you bring your elbow up and cock your arm before throwing the backfist. This is not wrong, however it does give our opponent a signal that something is about to happen. We can remove the signal; again, do not move the elbow first. Second, the fist must move in a straight line. The traditional way of throwing the backfist is to throw it as if your elbow and arm were a hinge. This makes the movement too mechanical. There should not be any arc in the line that the hand will travel during the execution of the backfist technique.

Third, the distance between you and your opponent must be closed as fast as possible. The way to accomplish this is, your hand must move *FIRST*. It has long been thought that if you move the body before or at the same time you throw the backfist, you will achieve maximum efficiency. It has been my experience that this is not, in fact, the case. If you want to hit your opponent consistently, the hand must move first and the body will follow. All movements with the fist should be whipping, snapping movements. To accomplish this you must keep your wrist relaxed and loose. Do not make a real tight fist, it will slow down your backfist.

KUNG-FU CROSS

DEFENSE AGAINST: LEFT PUNCH

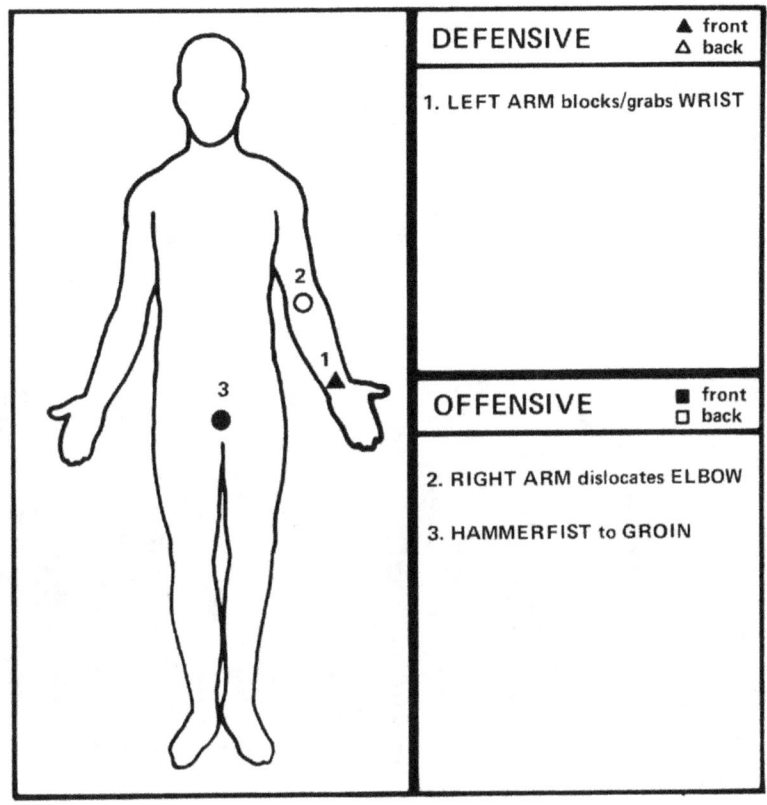

KUNG—FU CROSS

1 natural position

2 right foot to 5:30, left upward block

5 bring right arm to attacker's right elbow

6 hyperextend attacker's left elbow

NOTE: photo 3
This block is not done hard. If you block the strike upward with too much force, it will make it very difficult to execute the wrist grab.

DEFENSE AGAINST: LEFT PUNCH

3 left hand grabs attacker's wrist

4 right foot to 11:30

7 begin right hammerfist to the groin

8 right hammerfist to the groin

DIVIDED SWORD

DEFENSE AGAINST: RIGHT STEP-THROUGH PUNCH

2

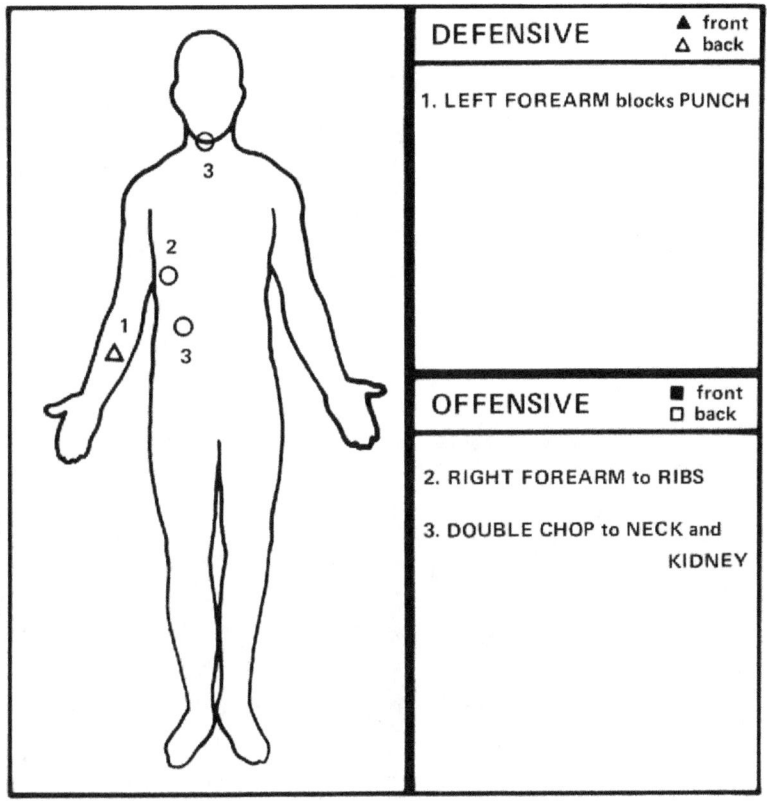

DEFENSIVE	▲ front △ back

1. LEFT FOREARM blocks PUNCH

OFFENSIVE	■ front □ back

2. RIGHT FOREARM to RIBS

3. DOUBLE CHOP to NECK and KIDNEY

DIVIDED SWORD

1 ready position

2 left foot to 10:30, begin left inward punch

5 right forearm to attacker's ribs

6 right elbow passes through ribs

Note: Be sure to keep knees bent on this technique in order to maintain control.

DEFENSE AGAINST: RIGHT STEP-THROUGH PUNCH

3 left block to punch

4 right elbow begins to come around

7 right chop, left chop ready position

8 right chop to attacker's neck, left chop his kidney

ARM HOOK

DEFENSE AGAINST: RIGHT STEP-THROUGH PUNCH

3

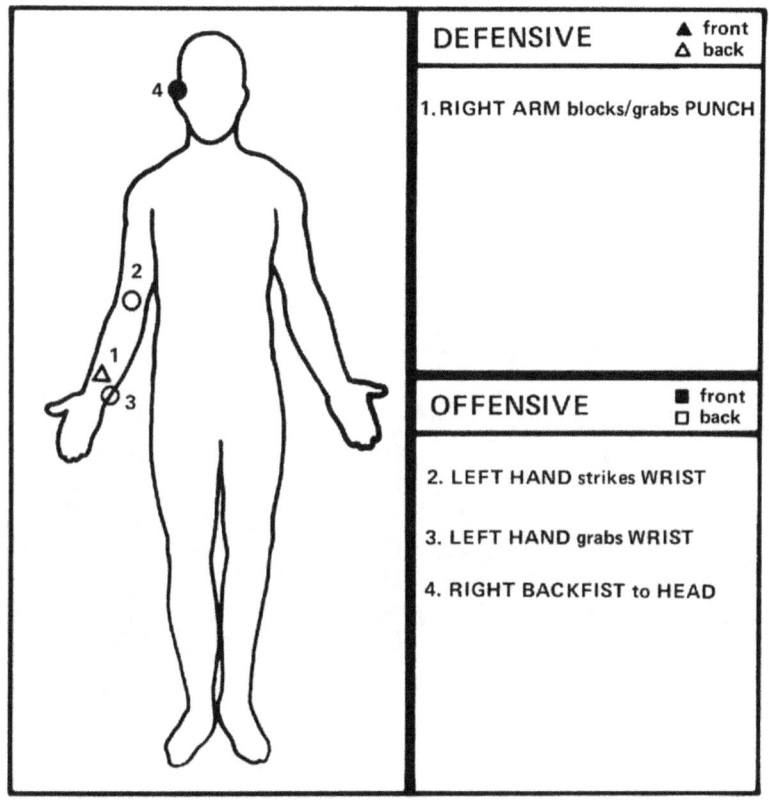

DEFENSIVE ▲ front △ back

1. RIGHT ARM blocks/grabs PUNCH

OFFENSIVE ■ front □ back

2. LEFT HAND strikes WRIST
3. LEFT HAND grabs WRIST
4. RIGHT BACKFIST to HEAD

ARM HOOK

1 ready position

2 left foot to 10:30

5 grab his wrist

6 begin left hand strike to attacker's elbow

9 left foot to 6:30

10 pull attacker towards you

NOTE: photos 3-9 When you step up to 10:30 with your left foot, it is not a permanent step. It is a transitional move only. The second step to 6:30 is the final step.

DEFENSE AGAINST: RIGHT STEP-THROUGH PUNCH

3 right extended outward block

4 begin grabbing attacker's wrist

7 strike elbow with left hand

8 bring left hand down attacker's arm to grab his wrist

11 ready the right hand for backfist

12 backfist to his head

CROSSING THE SUN

DEFENSE AGAINST: OVERHEAD CLUB ATTACK

4

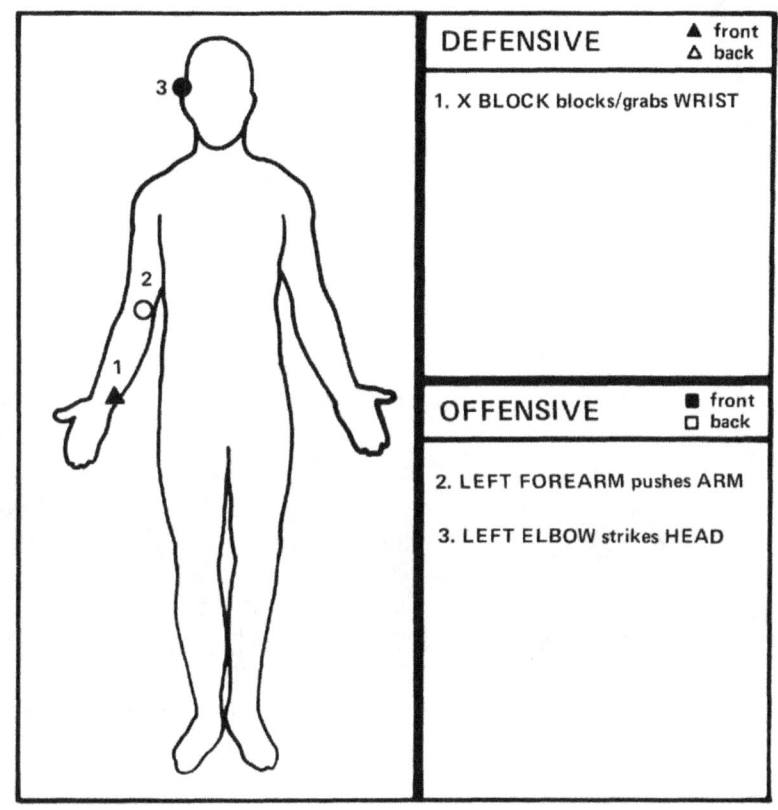

DEFENSIVE ▲ front / △ back

1. X BLOCK blocks/grabs WRIST

OFFENSIVE ■ front / □ back

2. LEFT FOREARM pushes ARM
3. LEFT ELBOW strikes HEAD

CROSSING THE SUN

1 ready position

2 left foot to 10:30, begin overhead X block

5 left forearm on attacker's right elbow

6 left hand ready position to push attacker's elbow

9 left elbow in ready position

10 left elbow strikes attacker on the side of head

DEFENSE AGAINST: OVERHEAD CLUB ATTACK

3 X block

4 right hand counter-grabs attacker's wrist

7 force attacker down with left forearm

8 force attacker down with left forearm

NOTE: photos 2-3
As you step to 10:30 with your left foot and overhead X block, be sure to move your head to the left to insure that you will not be struck in the head on club follow through.

OPENING THE FAN

DEFENSE AGAINST: RIGHT STEP-THROUGH PUNCH

5

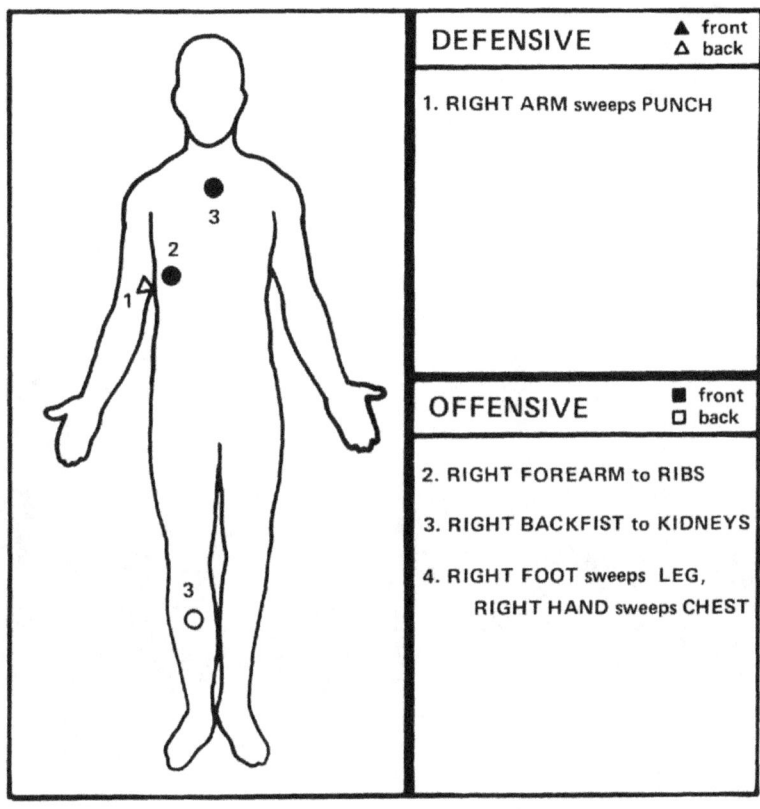

DEFENSIVE ▲ front △ back

1. RIGHT ARM sweeps PUNCH

OFFENSIVE ■ front □ back

2. RIGHT FOREARM to RIBS
3. RIGHT BACKFIST to KIDNEYS
4. RIGHT FOOT sweeps LEG, RIGHT HAND sweeps CHEST

1 ready position

OPENING THE FAN

2 left hand begins parry

3 right sweeping upper block on attacker's punching arm

6 right forearm to attacker's ribs

7 right forearm goes through attacker's ribs

10 right hand sweeps attacker's chest as your right foot sweeps his front leg

11 attacker goes down

NOTE: photos 2-4 The right sweeping upward block is to be one continuous movement. Do not stop.

DEFENSE AGAINST: RIGHT STEP-THROUGH PUNCH

4 right sweeping upper block continues up and down

5 right forearm ready position

8 right back fist to attacker's kidneys

9 right foot steps behind attacker's right foot

12 attacker continues to go down

13 attacker defenseless on the ground

WING BREAK

DEFENSE AGAINST: SHOULDER GRAB FROM RIGHT SIDE

6

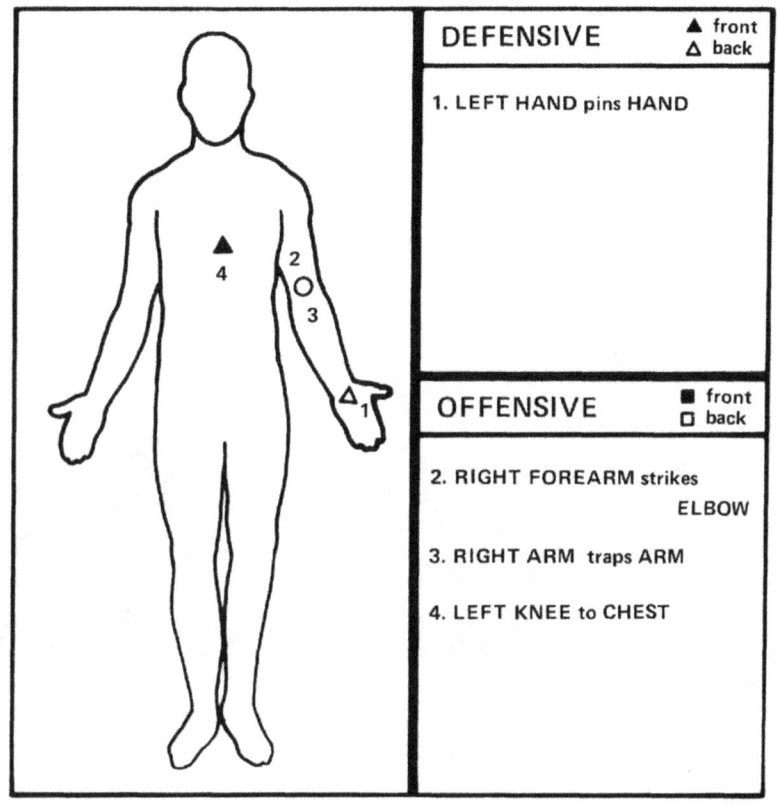

DEFENSIVE ▲ front △ back

1. LEFT HAND pins HAND

OFFENSIVE ■ front □ back

2. RIGHT FOREARM strikes ELBOW

3. RIGHT ARM traps ARM

4. LEFT KNEE to CHEST

WING BREAK

1 ready position

2 right foot to 3:00

5 right hand begins counter-clockwise movement over attacker's left arm

6 right arm continues over his arm

9 left foot to 6:00

10 force attacker around

NOTE: photos 9-10 After you wrap your arm around his back it is very

DEFENSE AGAINST: SHOULDER GRAB FROM RIGHT SIDE

3 left hand pins attacker's left hand

4 right forearm strikes attacker's left elbow

7 right arm wraps under attacker's arm

8 right arm grabs attacker's back

11 continue forcing attacker around and over

12 left knee to attacker's chest

important to drop into a low stance in order to pull him around into a knee strike.

DARKNESS

DEFENSE AGAINST: RIGHT STEP-THROUGH PUNCH FROM RIGHT SIDE

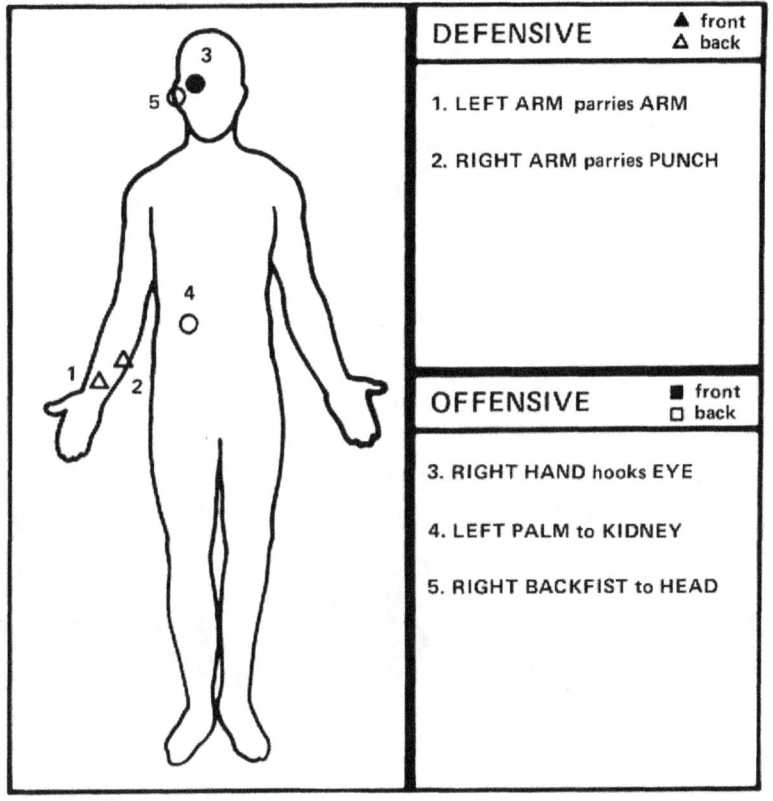

DEFENSIVE ▲ front / △ back

1. LEFT ARM parries ARM
2. RIGHT ARM parries PUNCH

OFFENSIVE ■ front / □ back

3. RIGHT HAND hooks EYE
4. LEFT PALM to KIDNEY
5. RIGHT BACKFIST to HEAD

DARKNESS

1 ready position

2 right foot to 9:00

5 right hand checks attacker's punching arm

6 left foot steps to 7:30

9 throwing right back fist

10 back fist to attacker's head

DEFENSE AGAINST: RIGHT STEP-THROUGH PUNCH FROM RIGHT SIDE

3 left parry

4 right parry

7 right hand hooks attacker's eye

8 left palm strike to attacker's kidney

NOTE: photos 2-4
This block is NOT a hard one. It does not stop the punch, but redirects the punch past your head.

FLASHING WINGS

DEFENSE AGAINST: RIGHT STEP-THROUGH PUNCH

8

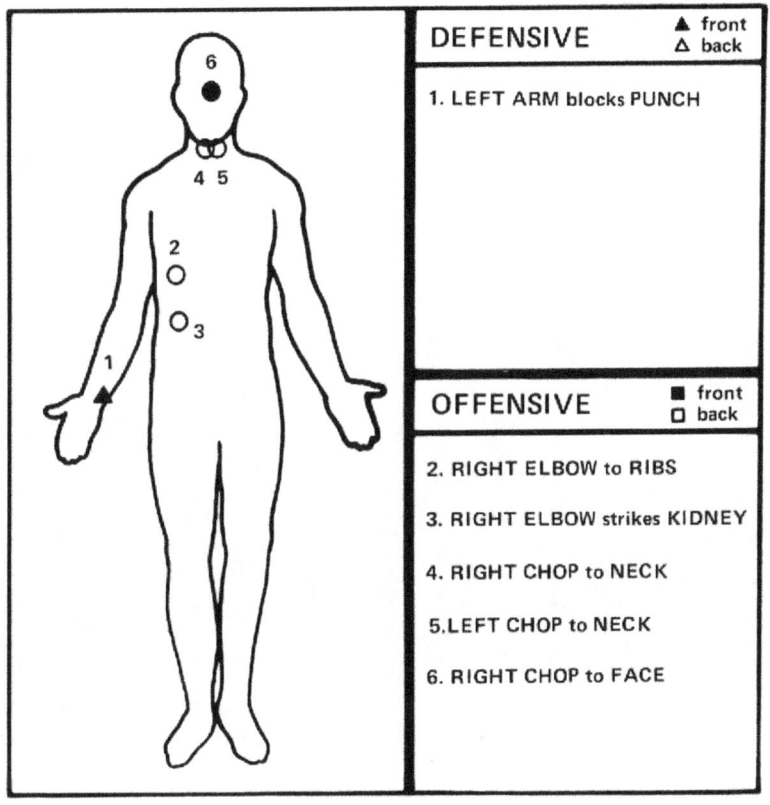

DEFENSIVE   ▲ front
                △ back

1. LEFT ARM blocks PUNCH

OFFENSIVE   ■ front
                □ back

2. RIGHT ELBOW to RIBS
3. RIGHT ELBOW strikes KIDNEY
4. RIGHT CHOP to NECK
5. LEFT CHOP to NECK
6. RIGHT CHOP to FACE

FLASHING WINGS

1 ready position

2 left foot to 11:30
left block attacker's punch

5 right elbow strikes attacker's kidney

6 right hand chop ready position
left hand chop ready position

9 left chop to attacker's neck

10 driving left chop through attacker's
neck driving attacker down

Note: photos 3-5 When you strike his ribs with your right elbow, be sure to turn

DEFENSE AGAINST: RIGHT STEP-THROUGH PUNCH

3 right elbow to attacker's ribs

4 right elbow ready position

7 right chop attacker's neck

8 left hand ready position

11 right chop ready position

12 right chop attacker's face

counter-clockwise at the waist to generate maximum power and to prepare yourself for the next movement.

SNAPPING TWIG

DEFENSE AGAINST: LEFT HAND TO RIGHT LAPEL GRAB

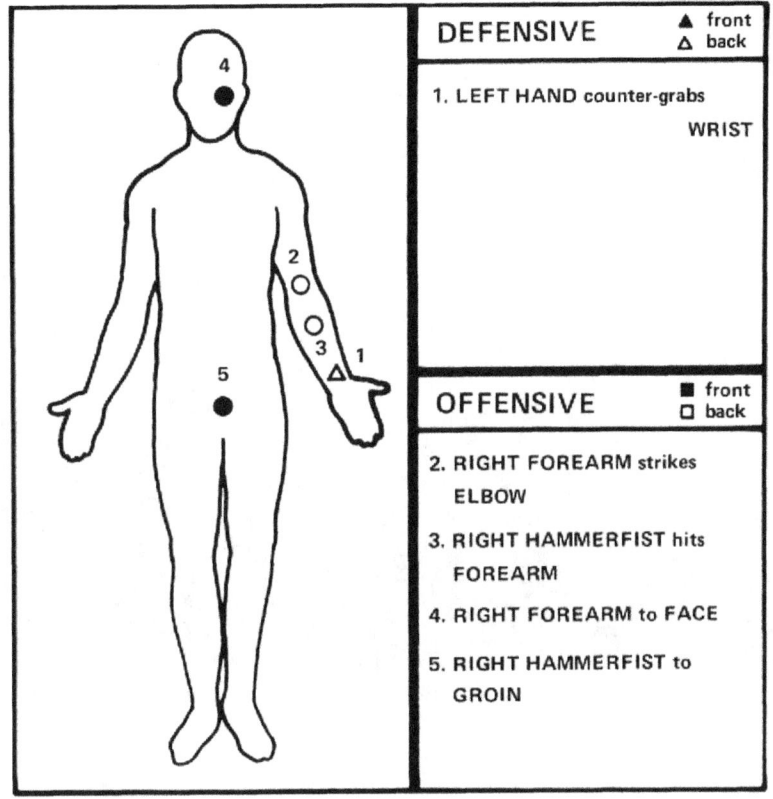

DEFENSIVE ▲ front / △ back

1. LEFT HAND counter-grabs
   WRIST

OFFENSIVE ■ front / □ back

2. RIGHT FOREARM strikes ELBOW
3. RIGHT HAMMERFIST hits FOREARM
4. RIGHT FOREARM to FACE
5. RIGHT HAMMERFIST to GROIN

SNAPPING TWIG

1 ready position

2 left hand counter-grabs attacker's left wrist

5 right hammerfist ready position

6 knock attacker's hand off lapel

9 right forearm to attacker's face

10 begin hammerfist ready position

Note: photos 6-9 After you strike his elbow, it is important to remember the knock off, the four knuckle rake, and the forearm movement. These

DEFENSE AGAINST: LEFT HAND TO RIGHT LAPEL GRAB

3 left foot to 6:30, right hammerfist ready position

4 strike attacker's elbow with right forearm strike

7 drive arm down

8 right forearm in ready position

11 right hammerfist in ready position in kneeling stance

12 right hammerfist to attacker's groin

are three continuous circular movements, just like you are making circles with your right arm.

PRAYER OF DEATH

DEFENSE AGAINST: RIGHT SNAP KICK WHILE IN KNEELING POSITION

10

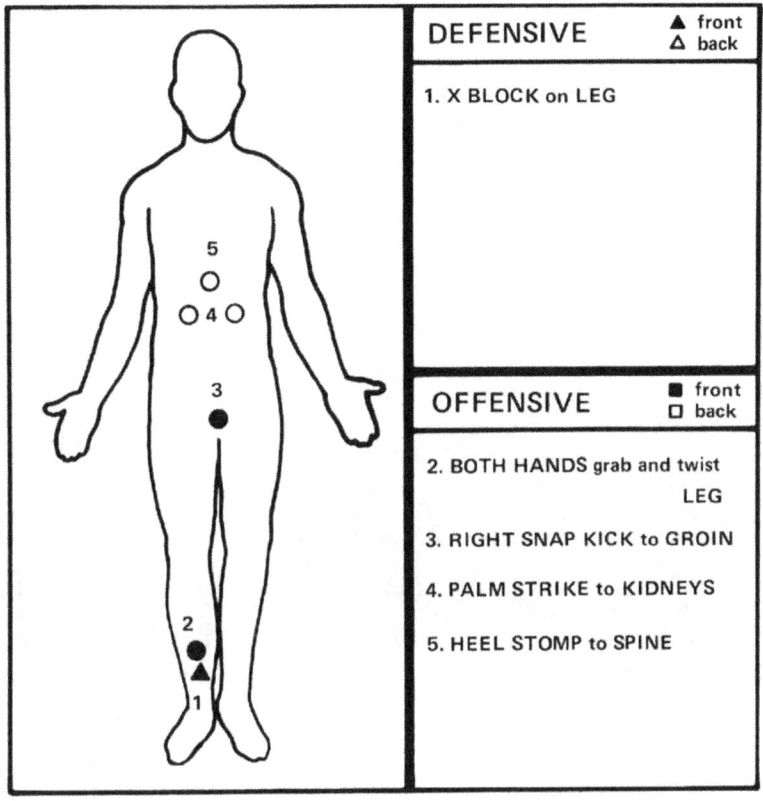

DEFENSIVE ▲ front / △ back

1. X BLOCK on LEG

OFFENSIVE ■ front / □ back

2. BOTH HANDS grab and twist LEG
3. RIGHT SNAP KICK to GROIN
4. PALM STRIKE to KIDNEYS
5. HEEL STOMP to SPINE

PRAYER OF DEATH

1 ready position

2 attacker comes in with kick, ready position for X block on attacker's leg

5 turn foot

6 turning attacker around by twisting foot, begin coming up

9 release his foot, ready position striking kidneys with palm strike

10 palm strike knocks attacker down

DEFENSE AGAINST: RIGHT SNAP KICK WHILE IN KNEELING POSITION

3 X block on attacker's leg

4 right hand grabs attacker's heel, left hand grabs top of his foot

7 standing up, ready position for right snap kick

8 right snap kick to the groin

11 ready position for heel stomp to attacker's spine

12 stomp to attacker's back

the kick as opposed to deflecting it.

RISING KICK

DEFENSE AGAINST: RIGHT STEP-THROUGH PUNCH

11

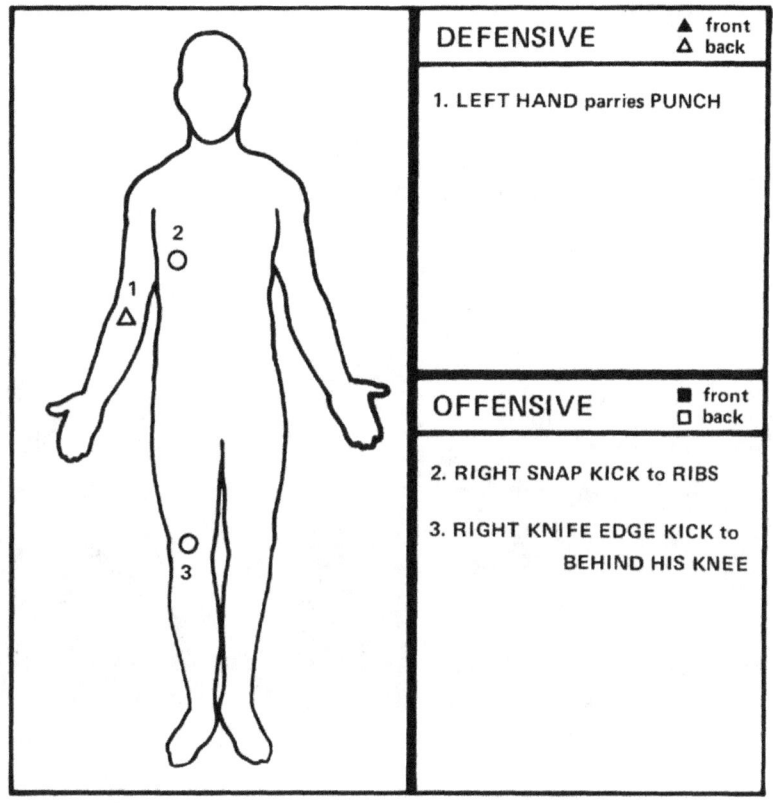

DEFENSIVE ▲ front / △ back

1. LEFT HAND parries PUNCH

OFFENSIVE ■ front / □ back

2. RIGHT SNAP KICK to RIBS

3. RIGHT KNIFE EDGE KICK to BEHIND HIS KNEE

RISING KICK

1 ready position

2 left foot to 9:00

5 right snap kick to the ribs

6 right knife edge kick ready position

DEFENSE AGAINST: RIGHT STEP-THROUGH PUNCH

3 left hand parries the punch

4 right snap kick ready position

7 right knife edge to behind of attacker's right knee

8 collapsing him to the floor

NOTE: photos 6-8

The kick to his right knee is not a snapping kick, it is a thrusting kick driving through his knee.

CIRCLE OF CHINA

DEFENSE AGAINST: RIGHT SNAP KICK WHILE IN KNEELING POSITION

12

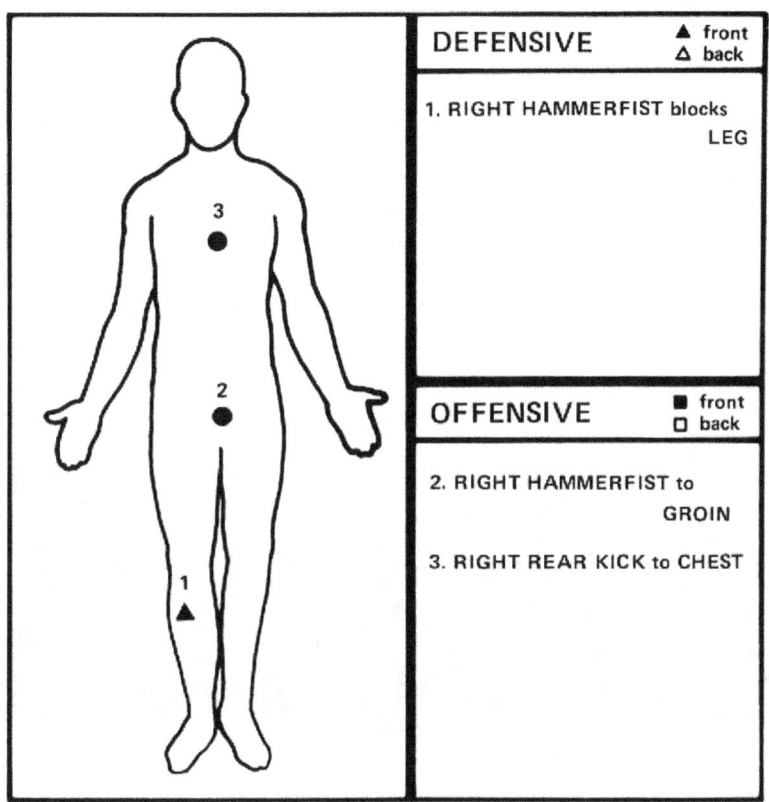

DEFENSIVE ▲ front △ back

1. RIGHT HAMMERFIST blocks LEG

OFFENSIVE ■ front □ back

2. RIGHT HAMMERFIST to GROIN

3. RIGHT REAR KICK to CHEST

CIRCLE OF CHINA

1 ready position

2 right hammerfist ready position to block attacker's kick

4 begin turning on your left knee to ready position for hammerfist

5 hammerfist in ready position

7 hands on the floor as you lean away from attacker

8 right rear kick to attacker's chest

DEFENSE AGAINST: RIGHT SNAP KICK WHILE IN KNEELING POSITION

3 right hammerfist blocking attacker's kick

NOTE: photos 1-9
Be sure to keep your head down and eyes on his kick. It is hard enough to block a hard kick that you can see. It is impossible to block it if you don't see it.

6 hammerfist to attacker's groin

9 pull kick back

OPENING COWL

13

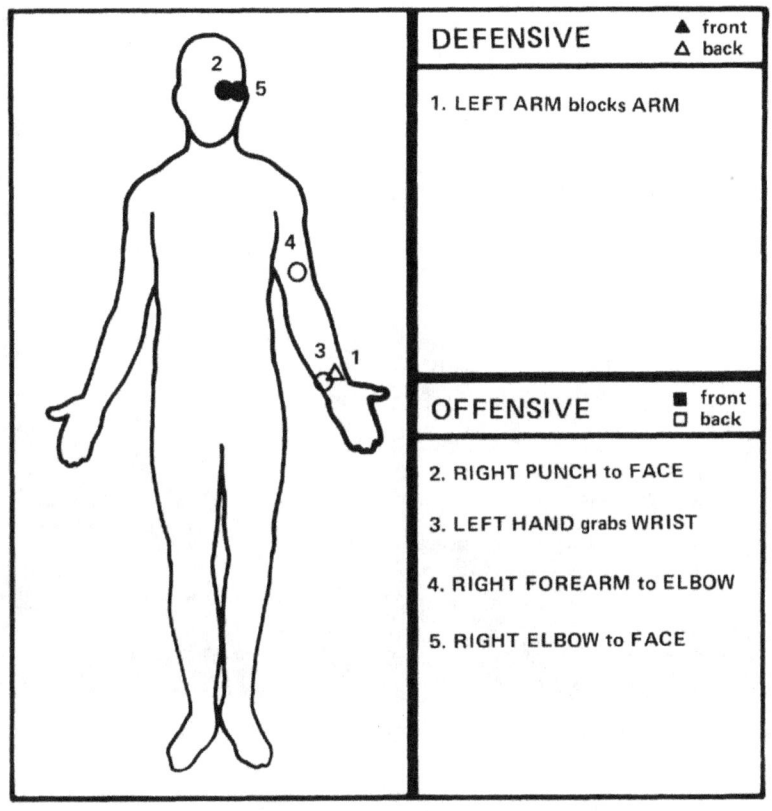

DEFENSIVE ▲ front △ back

1. LEFT ARM blocks ARM

OFFENSIVE ■ front □ back

2. RIGHT PUNCH to FACE
3. LEFT HAND grabs WRIST
4. RIGHT FOREARM to ELBOW
5. RIGHT ELBOW to FACE

OPENING COWL

1 ready position

2 left foot to 5:30

5 left hand grabbing attacker's wrist

6 right forearm on attacker's left elbow

9 right elbow ready position

10 right elbow to side of attacker's face

DEFENSE AGAINST: TWO-HAND CHOKE FROM BEHIND

3 left outward block

4 right punch to face

7 right foot stepping straight forward

8 forcing attacker down with forearm

NOTE: photos 4-5

Be sure not to over extend your left outward block since it will make it very difficult to grab his left wrist if you push it too far to the left.

STICKS OF SATAN

DEFENSE AGAINST: OVERHEAD CLUB ATTACK

14

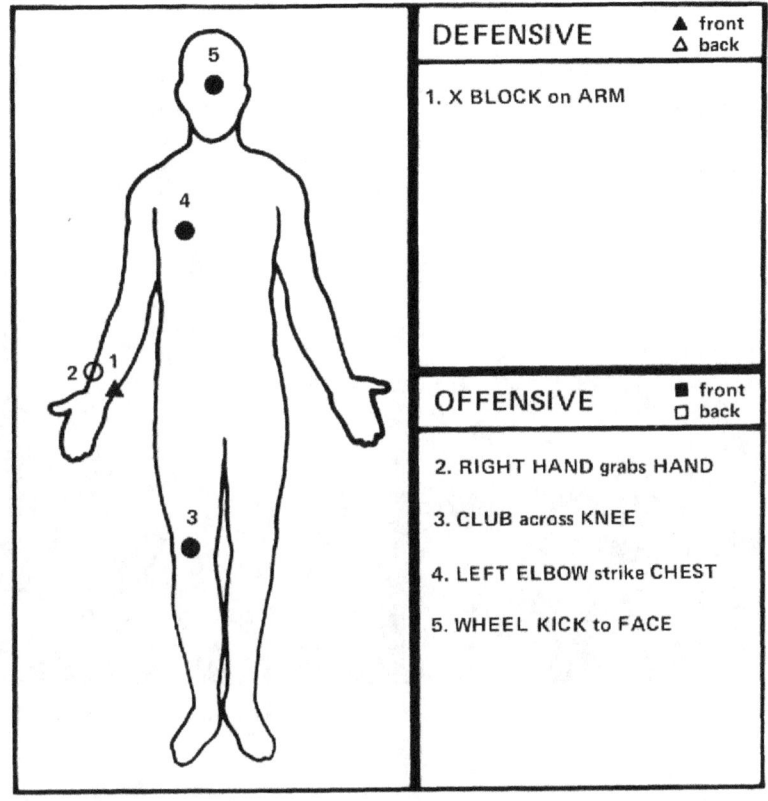

DEFENSIVE ▲ front / △ back

1. X BLOCK on ARM

OFFENSIVE ■ front / □ back

2. RIGHT HAND grabs HAND
3. CLUB across KNEE
4. LEFT ELBOW strike CHEST
5. WHEEL KICK to FACE

STICKS OF SATAN

1 ready position

2 left foot to 10:30, X block ready position

5 bring club down

6 bring club across attacker's knee

9 right foot to 5:30

10 ready position to throw attacker's arm straight down

Note: photos 10-11 When you throw his right hand down in the last movement,

DEFENSE AGAINST: OVERHEAD CLUB ATTACK

3 X block blocking overhead club attack

4 right hand grabs the club hand of the attacker

7 right foot to 11:00

8 left elbow strike to attacker's chest

11 snapping attacker's arm with club straight down

12 wheel kick to attacker's face

be sure to SNAP his entire arm down in order to expose his head for the kick. The head will react as in a whiplash.

DANCER

DEFENSE AGAINST: TWO HAND CHOKE FROM BEHIND

15

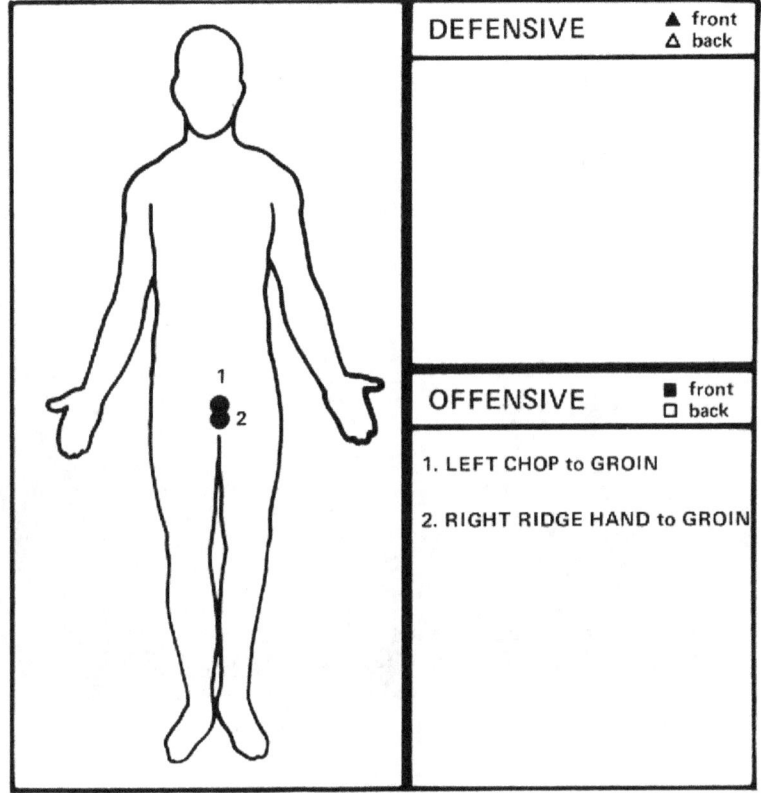

DEFENSIVE ▲ front △ back

OFFENSIVE ■ front □ back

1. LEFT CHOP to GROIN

2. RIGHT RIDGE HAND to GROIN

DANCER

1 ready position

2 left foot to 3:30

4 left chop to attacker's groin

5 right ridge hand ready position

7 right ridge hand to attacker's groin

8 spinning out to right foot 3:00 position

DEFENSE AGAINST: TWO-HAND CHOKE FROM BEHIND

3 left hand ready chop position

6 right ridge hand ready position

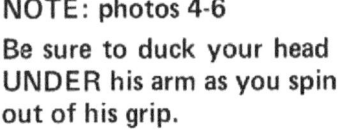

NOTE: photos 4-6
Be sure to duck your head UNDER his arm as you spin out of his grip.

9 fighting stance

THE BRIDGE

DEFENSE AGAINST: TWO HAND CHOKE FROM BEHIND

16

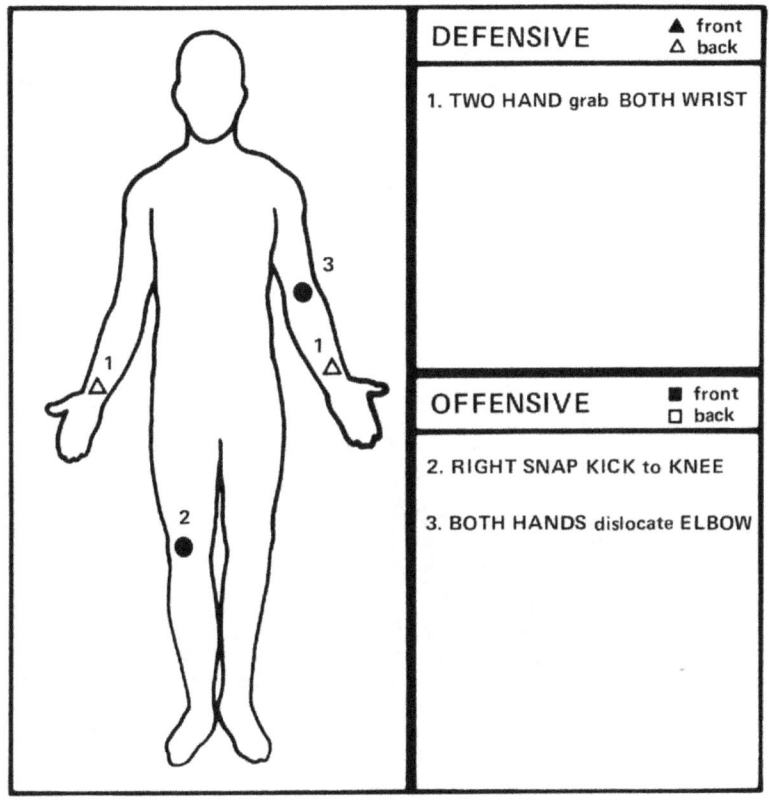

DEFENSIVE ▲ front △ back

1. TWO HAND grab BOTH WRIST

OFFENSIVE ■ front □ back

2. RIGHT SNAP KICK to KNEE

3. BOTH HANDS dislocate ELBOW

THE BRIDGE

1 ready position

2 left foot to 9:00

5 grab attacker's wrist

6 right foot to 9:00 as you bring attacker's hands off your neck

9 right snap kick ready position

10 right snap kick to attacker's knee

NOTE: photos 11-12 When you cross his arms, be sure to PULL your left

DEFENSE AGAINST: TWO-HAND CHOKE FROM BEHIND

3 both hands in ready position to grab attacker's wrist

4 continuing both hands in ready position to grab attacker's wrist

7 attacker's arms will be crossed

8 twisting attacker's arms right

11 snapping arms

12 break elbow

arm as you push your right arm. This will increase your leverage.

ROCKING ELBOW

DEFENSE AGAINST: LEFT HAND GRAB TO RIGHT WRIST

17

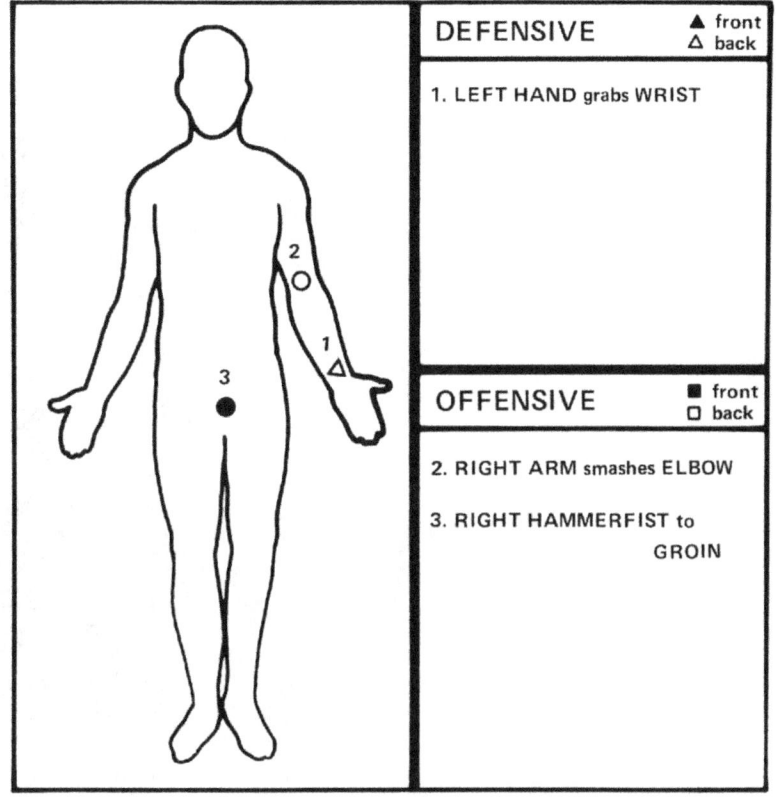

DEFENSIVE ▲ front / △ back

1. LEFT HAND grabs WRIST

OFFENSIVE ■ front / □ back

2. RIGHT ARM smashes ELBOW

3. RIGHT HAMMERFIST to GROIN

ROCKING ELBOW

1 ready position

3 right foot to 11:30

NOTE: photos 3-4
Turn your right shoulder into his elbow as you pull his left arm into you to break his elbow.

DEFENSE AGAINST: LEFT HAND GRAB TO RIGHT WRIST

2 left hand grabs attacker's left wrist

4 right arm smashes attacker's left elbow

5 right hammerfist to groin

AIMING THE SPEAR

DEFENSE AGAINST: LEFT HAND TO RIGHT LAPEL GRAB

18

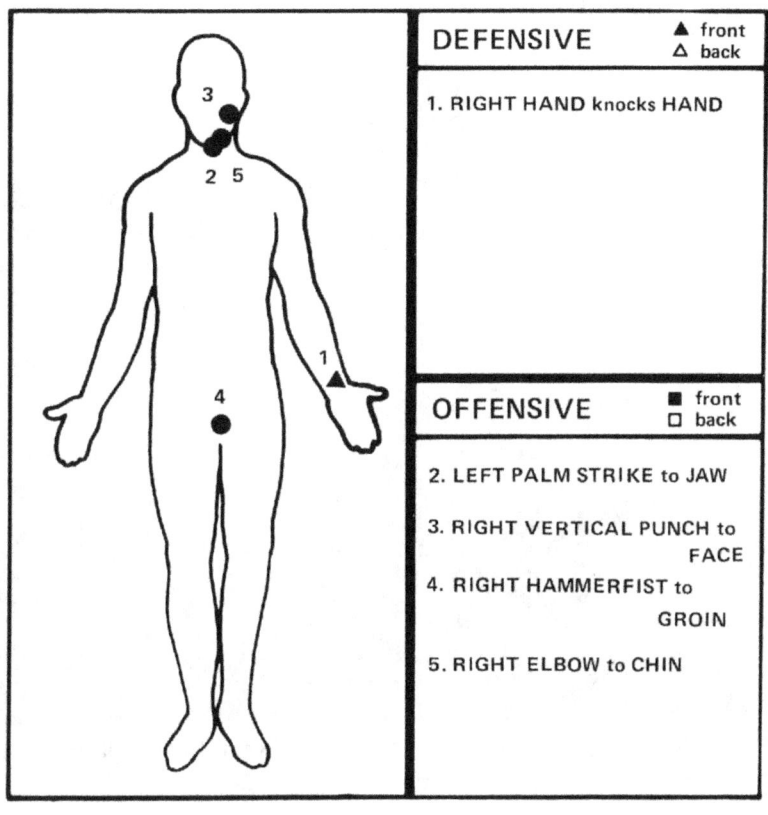

DEFENSIVE ▲ front △ back

1. RIGHT HAND knocks HAND

OFFENSIVE ■ front □ back

2. LEFT PALM STRIKE to JAW
3. RIGHT VERTICAL PUNCH to FACE
4. RIGHT HAMMERFIST to GROIN
5. RIGHT ELBOW to CHIN

AIMING THE SPEAR

1 ready position

2 right hand ready position for outward block strike

4 left foot to 11:00, left palm strike to attacker's jaw at the same time

5 right vertical punch to attacker's face

7 right hammerfist to attacker's groin

8 right elbow ready position

DEFENSE AGAINST: LEFT HAND TO RIGHT LAPEL GRAB

3 right hand knocks attacker's hand off your lapel

NOTE: photos 3-4
Movements are to be done simultaneously

6 right hammerfist ready position

9 right elbow to attacker's chin

U-PUNCH

DEFENSE AGAINST: TWO HAND CHOKE OR LAPEL GRAB FROM FRONT

19

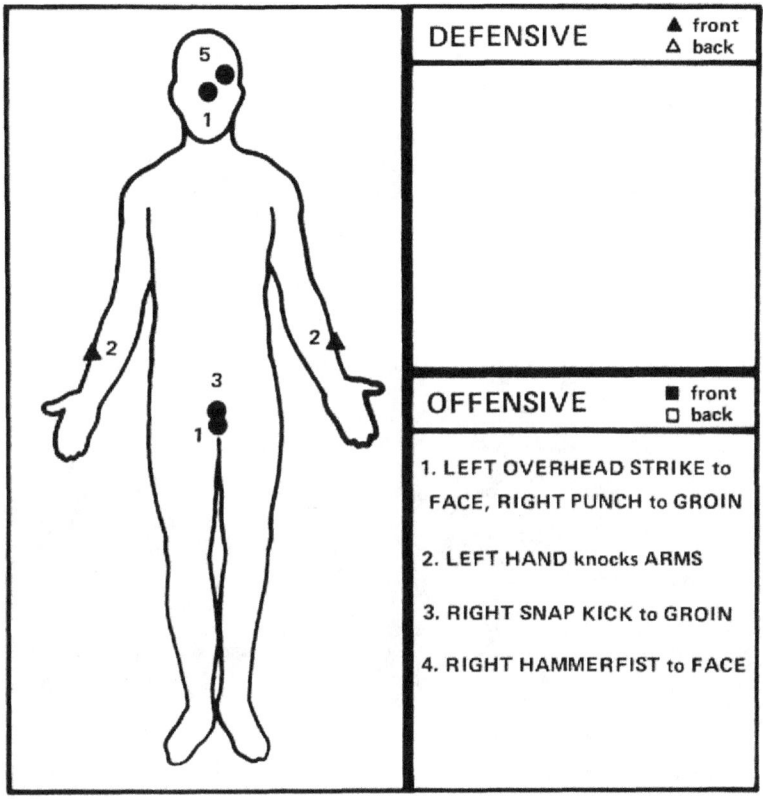

DEFENSIVE ▲ front
△ back

OFFENSIVE ■ front
□ back

1. LEFT OVERHEAD STRIKE to FACE, RIGHT PUNCH to GROIN

2. LEFT HAND knocks ARMS

3. RIGHT SNAP KICK to GROIN

4. RIGHT HAMMERFIST to FACE

U PUNCH

1 ready position

2 right foot to 12:00

5 left hand ready position to knock attacker's arms off

6 right foot drawing back into cat stance as left hand knocks arms off

9 stepping forward to 11:00 position with right foot, right hammerfist ready

10 right hammerfist to side of attacker's face

DEFENSE AGAINST: TWO-HAND CHOKE OR LAPEL GRIP FROM FRONT

3 left overhead punch, right under punch ready position

4 left overhead punch to face, right under punch to attacker's groin

7 right snap kick to groin

8 snapping right kick back

NOTE: photos 5-6

Be sure to knock his arms down and OFF. Don't pull him into you.

UNCOVERING THE FLAME

DEFENSE AGAINST: GUN IN CLOSE WITH HANDS UP

20

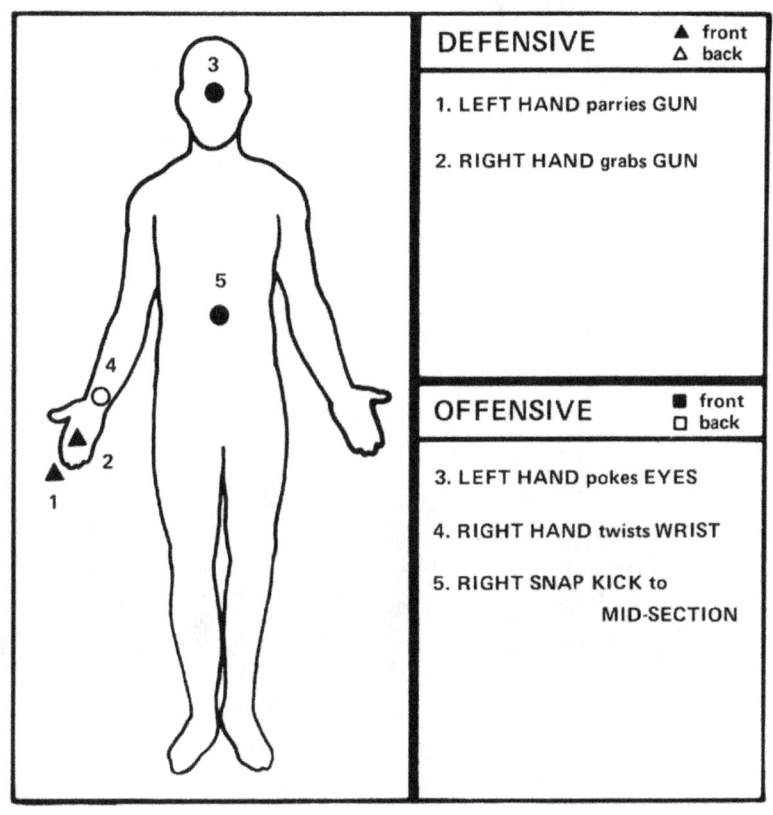

DEFENSIVE ▲ front
△ back

1. LEFT HAND parries GUN
2. RIGHT HAND grabs GUN

OFFENSIVE ■ front
□ back

3. LEFT HAND pokes EYES
4. RIGHT HAND twists WRIST
5. RIGHT SNAP KICK to MID-SECTION

UNCOVERING THE FLAME

1 ready position

2 left hand ready position for parry movement

5 left hand finger-poke ready position

6 left hand finger-poke to attacker's eyes

9 right step kick ready position

10 right snap kick to attacker's mid-section

DEFENSE AGAINST: GUN IN CLOSE WITH HANDS UP

3 left hand parries gun as right foot steps to 12:00

4 right hand grabs gun

7 right foot stepping to 5:30

8 right hand twists gun towards attacker's face

NOTE: photos 2-4

Your left hand MUST begin the parry before you step to 12:00 with your right foot. DO NOT strike his gun hand hard. We want to move the gun away from us, not discharge the weapon.

COVERING THE FLAME

DEFENSE AGAINST: GUN IN CLOSE WITH HANDS DOWN

21

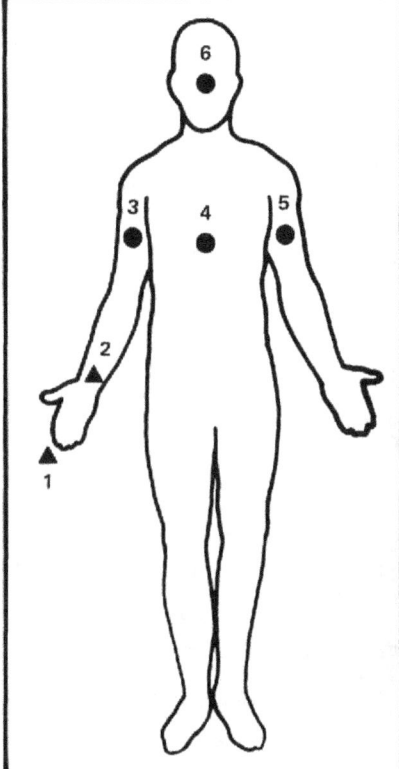

DEFENSIVE	▲ front △ back

1. RIGHT HAND parries GUN

2. LEFT HAND grabs WRIST, RIGHT FOREARM forces WRIST

OFFENSIVE	■ front □ back

3. RIGHT HEEL STOMP to BICEP

4. RIGHT HEEL STOMP to STERNUM

5. RIGHT HEEL STOMP to BICEP

6. RIGHT FINGER POKE to EYES

1 ready position

COVERING THE FLAME

2 right hand begins outward parry

3 left foot to 11:00, same time right hand parry

6 right foot to 10:30

7 force attacker down

10 right stomp attacker's sternum

11 right stomp ready position

NOTE: photos 7-12 Be certain to point his gun away from you after take-down

DEFENSE AGAINST: GUN IN CLOSE WITH HANDS DOWN

4 left hand grabs attacker's wrist

5 right forearm forces against attacker's right wrist

8 right heel stomp to attacker's bicep

9 right stomp ready position

12 right stomp left bicep

13 right finger poke to attacker's eyes

as you stomp his chest and arms.

DOUBLE BLADES

DEFENSE AGAINST: OVERHEAD CLUB ATTACK

22

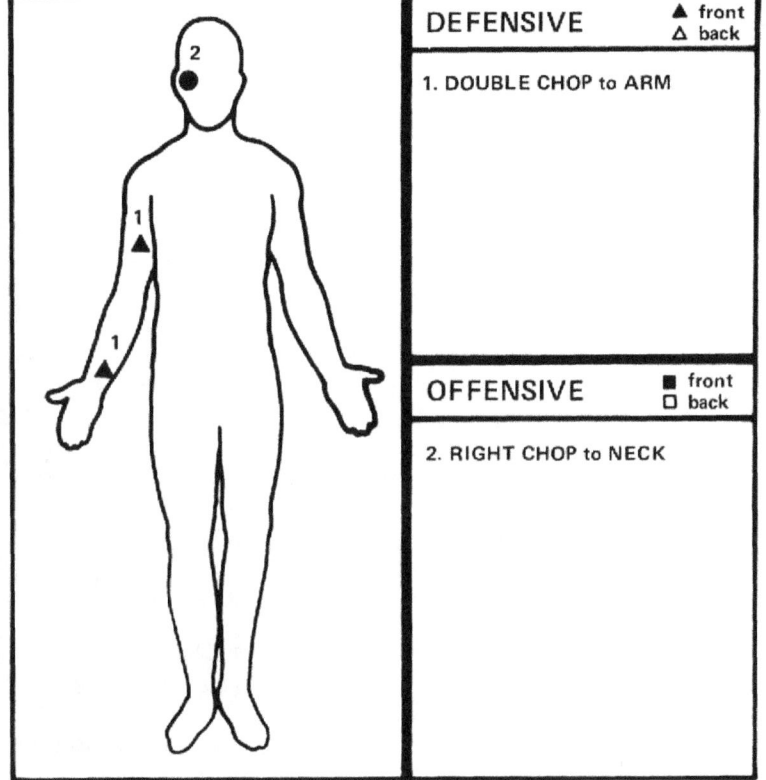

DEFENSIVE ▲ front △ back

1. DOUBLE CHOP to ARM

OFFENSIVE ■ front □ back

2. RIGHT CHOP to NECK

DOUBLE BLADES

1 ready position

3 both hands double chop ready position

5 left hand grabs attacker's wrist

DEFENSE AGAINST: OVERHEAD CLUB ATTACK

2 right foot to 12:00

4 left chop attacker's wrist, right chop to attacker's right bicep

NOTE: photo 4
Keep your head to the right during block so you will not be struck by club on follow through.

6 right hand a thrusting chop to attacker's neck

LEVELING THE CLOUDS

DEFENSE AGAINST: LEFT STEP-THROUGH PUNCH

23

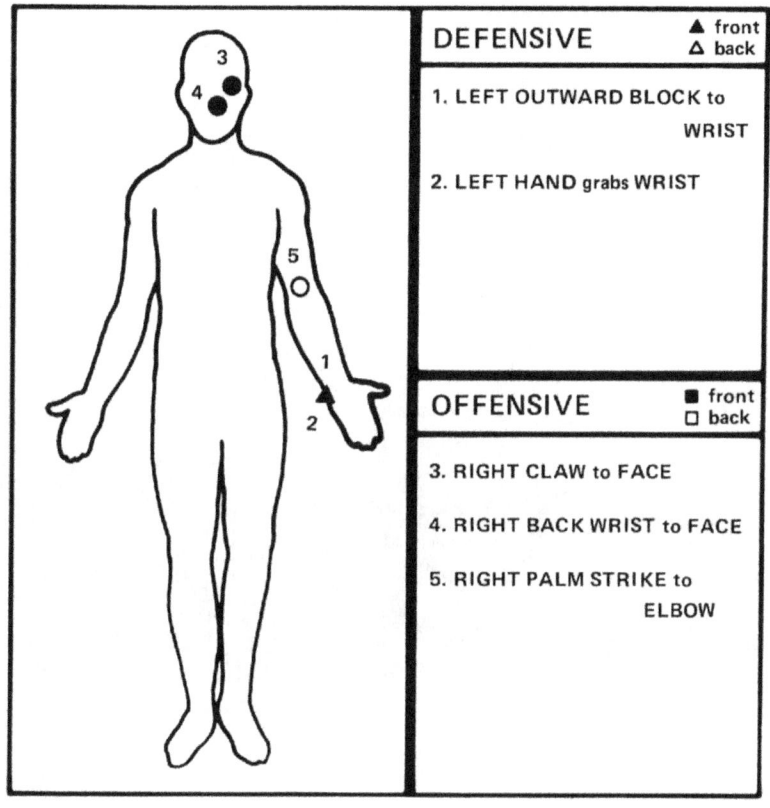

DEFENSIVE	▲ front △ back
1. LEFT OUTWARD BLOCK to WRIST	
2. LEFT HAND grabs WRIST	

OFFENSIVE	■ front □ back
3. RIGHT CLAW to FACE	
4. RIGHT BACK WRIST to FACE	
5. RIGHT PALM STRIKE to ELBOW	

LEVELING THE CLOUDS

1 ready position

2 right foot to 1:30, left extended outward block ready position

5 right claw to attacker's face

6 follow through with claw

9 right palm strike ready position

10 right palm strike to attacker's left elbow

DEFENSE AGAINST: LEFT STEP-THROUGH PUNCH

3 left extended outward block to attacker's left punch

4 a left hand grab to attacker's left wrist

7 right back wrist ready position

8 right back wrist to attacker's face

NOTE: photos 5-10
The movements are to be continuous flowing movements with no stops.

CIRCLES OF GLASS

DEFENSE AGAINST: RIGHT STEP-THROUGH PUNCH, LEFT PUNCH

24

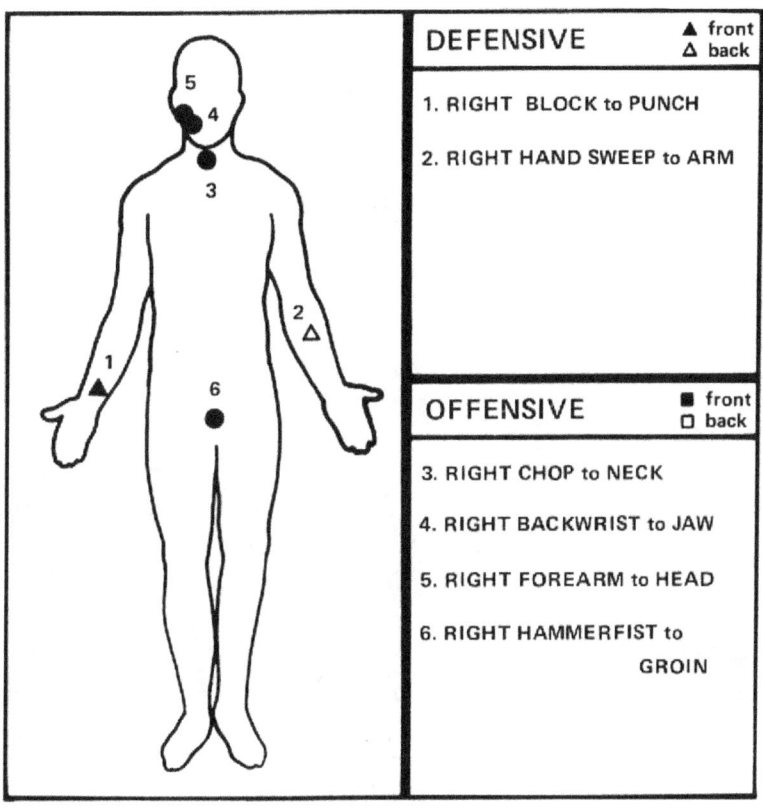

DEFENSIVE ▲ front / △ back

1. RIGHT BLOCK to PUNCH
2. RIGHT HAND SWEEP to ARM

OFFENSIVE ■ front / □ back

3. RIGHT CHOP to NECK
4. RIGHT BACKWRIST to JAW
5. RIGHT FOREARM to HEAD
6. RIGHT HAMMERFIST to GROIN

1 ready position

CIRCLES OF GLASS — DEFENSE

2 left foot to 6:00

3 right block to attacker's right punch

6 right hand chop ready position

7 right chop to attacker's neck

10 right forearm ready position

11 right forearm to attacker's head

NOTE: photos 8-13 Be sure to keep your knees bent during these multiple

AGAINST: RIGHT STEP-THROUGH PUNCH, LEFT PUNCH COMBINATION

4 left foot to 4:00 right sweep ready position

5 right sweep of left punch down

8 right back wrist ready position

9 left foot to 9:00, right back wrist to attacker's jaw

12 right forearm follow-through

13 right hammerfist to attacker's groin

movements in close technique. If you are not under control, you can't control your opponent.

FALLING HEEL

DEFENSE AGAINST: STEP-IN POKING KNIFE

25

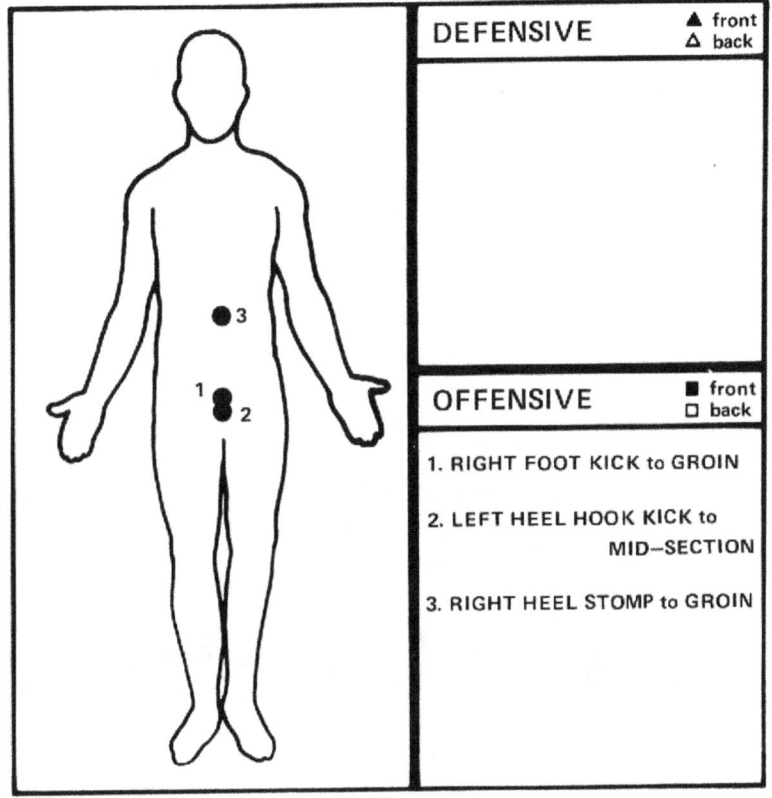

DEFENSIVE ▲ front
△ back

OFFENSIVE ■ front
□ back

1. RIGHT FOOT KICK to GROIN

2. LEFT HEEL HOOK KICK to MID-SECTION

3. RIGHT HEEL STOMP to GROIN

FALLING HEEL

1 ready position

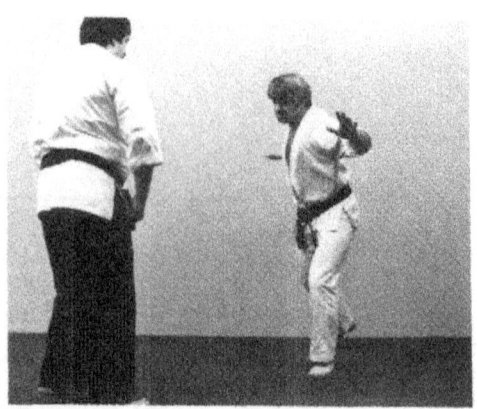

2 prepare to drop straight down to floor

5 ready position for right foot stepping behind attacker's right leg

6 begin roll

9 dropping attacker to the floor

10 right heel stomp ready position

DEFENSE AGAINST: STEP-IN POKING KNIFE

3 dropping to floor

4 right foot kick to attacker's groin

7 continuing roll

8 left heel hook kick to attacker's mid-section sweeping him over right leg

11 right heel stomp to attacker's groin

NOTE: photos 3-4
Very important TO DROP DOWN, not fall back on this ground technique. If you fall back you will be out of range for kick and take down.

THE SICKLE

DEFENSE AGAINST: RIGHT STEP-IN PUNCH

26

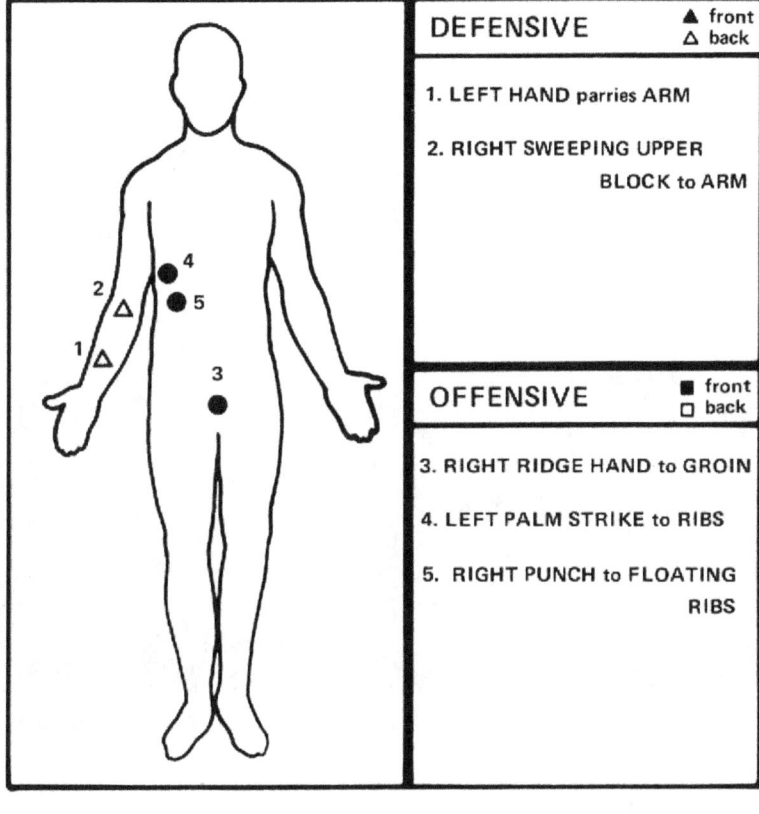

DEFENSIVE ▲ front △ back

1. LEFT HAND parries ARM
2. RIGHT SWEEPING UPPER BLOCK to ARM

OFFENSIVE ■ front □ back

3. RIGHT RIDGE HAND to GROIN
4. LEFT PALM STRIKE to RIBS
5. RIGHT PUNCH to FLOATING RIBS

THE SICKLE

1 ready position

2 ready position for left parry

5 right ridge hand ready position

6 right ridge hand to attacker's groin

9 right vertical punch ready position

10 right vertical punch to floating ribs

DEFENSE AGAINST: RIGHT STEP-IN PUNCH

3 left foot to 11:00, left hand parry

4 right sweeping upward block under the punch

7 left hand palm strike ready position

8 left hand palm strike to attacker's ribs

NOTE: photos 3-5

The sweeping upward block is to be done with snap. You want to get his arm up in order to create a large opening.

WATERFALL

DEFENSE AGAINST: RIGHT STEP-THROUGH PUNCH

27

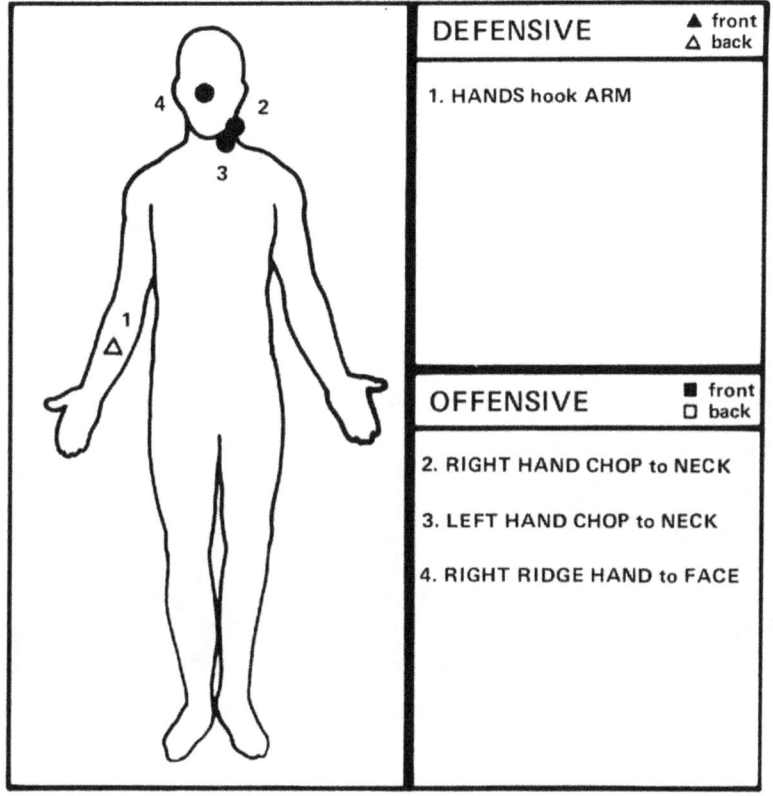

DEFENSIVE ▲ front △ back

1. HANDS hook ARM

OFFENSIVE ■ front □ back

2. RIGHT HAND CHOP to NECK
3. LEFT HAND CHOP to NECK
4. RIGHT RIDGE HAND to FACE

WATERFALL

1 ready position

2 left foot to 10:30, right sweeping block ready position

5 ready position for double chop

6 ready position double chop

9 right hand ready, ridge hand position

10 right ridge hand to attacker's face

DEFENSE AGAINST: RIGHT STEP-THROUGH PUNCH

3 hands hook punching arm

4 sweep attacker's punch down

7 right hand chops neck, left hand in ready position

8 left hand chops neck

NOTE: photos 3-5
As you block and sweep his punching arm down, the sweep down and double chop is one continuous movement.

A LEAP OF FAITH

What was the question facing Jay T. Will back in August of 1968; when as a 27 year old Black Belt still wet behind the ears, he decided to forego the final year of a football scholarship at San Jose State College, and open a Karate school. Encouraged, he wasn't. Friends warned that Ohio was nothing like California: "too conservative" they cautioned. He went ahead despite their well-intentioned advice and now marketing executives can add Karate to the list of goods and services introduced in the Midwest city, renowned as a "test market area" for U.S. products.

"The reason I picked Columbus," Will recalls, "was because I'm originally from Springfield, Ohio - my parents lived about 30 miles away. It was a wide-open town at the time. As far as I knew, there were only a couple of karate schools, small time affairs, and I felt that I could live with my parents until I got established, which was what I did." Years later, due to the interest he stirred in the area, "Will's Kenpo Karate" dojo was one of the most successful in the entire Midwest. But it didn't prosper simply because he sat there and waited for people to come in. Building on a solid tournament reputation (he held nearly every major title in the Ohio-Michigan countryside), he taught more than 200 students weekly, with the aid of five Brown Belts and one Black Belt. However, as Will liked to point out, "All that the shelf-full of trophies does is attract students. But once they come in, it's up to me to do a top notch job in order to keep them"

Opening "on the day the yellow pages were distributed," the most striking feature of the Jay T. Will Karate Studio was private instruction. "It's always been my intention to teach this way," he used to say, "since everyone takes Karate for a different reason, each is different physically and each person learns at a different rate." Instruction was available from ten in the morning until ten at night - six days a week. Students were also offered the option of attending group lessons and/or sparring classes, as part of what Will defined as a "combination program." Almost immediately, things just "took off"

("I don't know if I was in the right place at the right time, or what.") as enrollment soared, sparked by word-of-mouth and students defecting from other schools.

Before Will would recognize his interest in Karate, it took a coast guard reserve friend, Wayne Stevers, two months of constant harangue, two weddings (Stevers' and Will's) and one memorable stance. "Before he (Stevers) got out, I guess he started taking lessons at Ed Parker's school. And then from the time he got out, until I got out, he was always trying to talk me into taking Karate. I definitely remember him talking about it, but it went in one ear and out the other. I think it was in October of '65 when he got married; and when I went to his wedding, he was still bugging me about this karate. I just let it go and didn't say anything. Finally, I got married in November and he came to my wedding. Actually, it was a reception, and he got into this stance - it wasn't anything dramatic - and I said, 'Hey, that's neat; what is it?' He said, 'It's Karate. I've been telling you about it for two months but you've not been paying any attention.' I said, 'Well that's really neat? And that's what sparked my interest."

His military obligation behind him, Will elected to enroll at Santa Monica (Cal.) City College in January, 1966. Simultaneously, he began training at Ed Parker's school, also in Santa Monica, receiving instruction from Ed Parker and Scott Lorring.

By mid-August Will had received his Brown Belt, crediting his continued interest in the sport to Lorring. "He and I had a lot in common since he played football at Washington State. He had a big influence on my thinking; he believed in a rough and tumble type of thing, and that was what I had been exposed to through football and everything. That may not be the best type of Karate for everyone, but it turned out good for me." When he transferred to SJS after a year at SMCC, he continued his training under the supervision of Al Tracy and also got his first taste of tournament competition, nearly forfeiting his scholarship as a result! "The first tournament I fought in was the Central California Karate Championships held in Oceanside. That was during spring football practice and I broke my thumb.

I was really scared because you're not allowed to do anything like that when you're playing football on scholarship. If they catch you doing something you can get hurt at, they'll take it away. I couldn't tell them I broke my thumb and I had to go to practice on Monday. So I went through practice with a broken thumb and told them I broke it during practice." While still at San Jose State, Will was also exposed to the art of Kung-Fu by instructor Jerry Baumgarner.

"Jerry introduced me to a guy who was teaching out of his garage in San Mateo. I think he was teaching Hung-Gar, but I'm not sure. Anyway, he had been studying since he was nine and was an herbalist to boot. I studied with him for about a year and it was a great experience. You see, he would never charge me anything; all I had to do was go to the store and buy his whisky for him. He was 59, mind you, but could still do his stuff, despite the fact he was an alcoholic."

Shortly thereafter, armed only with his Black Belt, Will decided to set out on his own. Jay T. Will never regretted having forsaken a lackluster academic career in favor of Karate. BW (Before Will) martial enthusiasm in the Midwest had been lukewarm at best. Until his final days, he was highly regarded both as an instructor and promoter, having successfully defended his title at the Ohio Pro-Am for the final time in December, 1973.

What, if anything, did he glean during his tenure at SJS? "I don't feel that I got too much out of going to school, except the experience I received through communicating with other people. Back when I went to San Jose, Tommy Smith, Lee Evans and John Carlos were all students there. Tommy Smith was in one of my English classes, a basic composition class. Twice, he and I worked together on a paper. I remember one of them we had to write was on James Baldwin, the Black writer. He and I spent a lot of time together on that. We both had to write a paper, but one of us had to do an oral presentation. We flipped a coin and he lost. I got to know him pretty well because we often had to work together on projects. He's really a very sensitive guy; I like him very much. Ironically, he's the athletic director and track coach at Overland College in Ohio, which is only an hour from where I am." In recent months Will has expanded his litany of accomplishments to include the first and only accredited course at Ohio State - Me, a college dropout!" However, Will was disappointed with the results. "My class was the most popular phys. ed. course, but I didn't like it. I taught two sections that filled up 30 minutes after registration began, but people were taking it to fill a requirement." This, in his opinion, is no incentive. "People that aren't paying don't apply themselves. Two or three might practice on their own, but that's it. Most people refuse to apply themselves; I don't dig teaching that way at all."

Nonetheless, the class did blossom into a program on WOSU, an educational station operated by Ohio State. Will remembered, "I had my own show, aired twice daily, five days a week, with a different lesson weekly." The series was then picked up by the Ohio Educational Network and rerun this January through April on Mondays.

Will believed that the program ignited interest in Karate, while giving "every-body a lot of exposure."

When he was not teaching, promoting Karate or overseeing his various business ventures, Will pursued his favorite hobby as photographer for the Cincinnati Bengals program, Pro. "I'd like to become a recognized photographer but it's a very tough field. Again, though, I would only do it because I want to; not because my back is up against the wall." Will explained that he wanted to one day return to the Bay area of California. With financial security in the immediate future (due primarily to the fact that he ignored the predictions of soothsaying friends), he planed to continue teaching Karate, on a smaller, yet all encompassing scale.

From his vantage point at the time, Jay T. Will observed, "It's really a business management type thing for me now. I have to be there and keep on top of it. I have to make sure my instructors do things right." Although he only taught a few students a day, perhaps four or five: "In all honesty, it's harder now than when I was teaching for 12 hours a day."

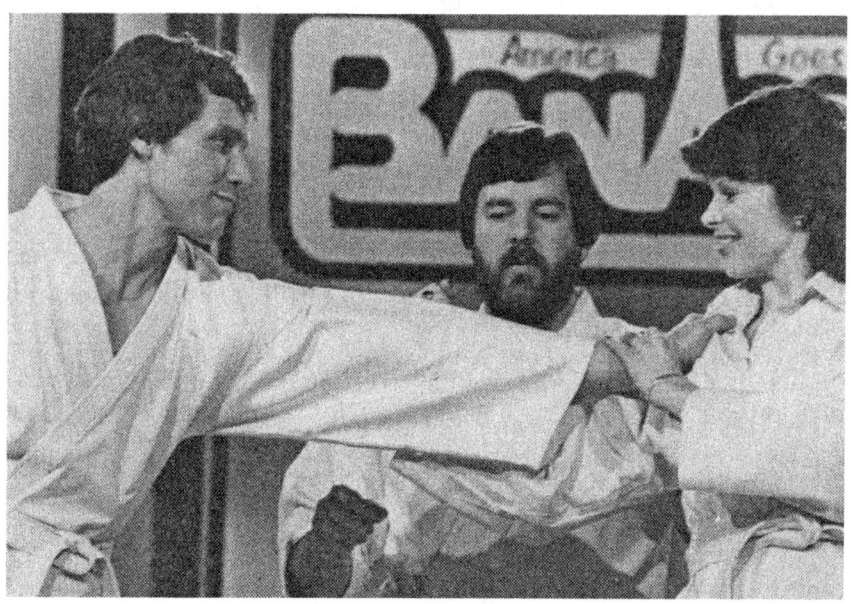

A NO-NONSENSE APPROACH TO KENPO

The Volkswagen pulls up to the curb and stops. A pick-up truck screeches to a halt from behind. A big, burly man jumps out of the truck, races up to the Volkswagen, rips open the door, and jerks out the young driver. Whap! The big man punches the kid. Whap! Whap!

Across from the curb, inside his karate studio, Jay T. Will looks up from his magazine. Through the window, he sees the kid ducking and avoiding the big man's punches, but with a minimum of success Jay gets up from his chair, walks over to his studio door, and calls out. "Hey, what's going on out there?"

"Butt out, man!" the big man says.

"Hey, you can smack that little kid around over nothing, but you can't do that same crap to me." Like a bull- dozer, he began to move steadily to- ward the man. Until suddenly, Jay found himself face to face with the black barrel of a .38 caliber handgun.

Years of martial arts training had prepared Jay for this moment. They all passed instantly before him the countless workouts, which developed reflexes and coordination the long hours of sparring with Joe Lewis, which perfected his uncanny technique and timing .the many sessions of meditation, which cultivated his immense inner strength. Jay was ready. There would be no hesitation. No indecision.

Calmly, Jay T. Will spun around on his heels and ... walked back into the studio

Two weeks later, the same big man who assaulted the kid, and who pulled the gun on Jay, made the front page of the local newspapers. He had gone home one night, drunk as usual, and pistol-whipped his wife. Later, after he fell asleep, his wife had picked up the .38 and shot him repeatedly through the head.

"So the moral of the story," declares Jay, "is that only one man ever pulled a gun on Jay T. Will. And two weeks later, he was dead!"

"Actually, the reason I tell that story is not for the humor, but because it illustrates several important points about self-defense. I mean that was a pretty serious situation. My life was in danger. And a half hour later, I was so scared that my hands were shaking."

Jay clapped his hands together and raised one massive fist like a club, "But that's the point I wasn't scared until a half hour later. A real self-defense situation happens right now. You don't have time to think about it, or to be scared. You just react. So that's the way you've got to train in the studio."

Many instructors argue that self- defense training begins with the formal exam. They believe that it is vital to put the student in a competitive environment, to force him to demonstrate his techniques before a large audience. Fear, they insist, is an adverse emotion which must be controlled, If a student cannot execute his techniques in the studio, under fear of the exam, how can he execute them on the street under fear of his life?

Jay T. Will, on the other hand, sees little value in this approach. "When you go out into a street situation, it's all now, and you react out of training You react out of instinct ... not sitting there thinking about it. And you don't have a two week, three week five day, or ten day build-up waiting for the examination. You're not going to develop all that anxiety."

"I don't care who you are - your best competitors in the world - Bill Wallace or Joe Lewis. You don't think they walk out into competition with nothing going on inside them? Their bodies prepare them for combat. The adrenalin starts pumping, and their muscles get ready So that's an anxiety situation. You're always thinking about what's coming or what's happening."

Instead, Jay teaches functional, usable, realistic self-defense. He does this by requiring his students to attend both group and private classes. There is no anxiety. The group classes give the students experience working with opponents of various heights and weights. But the private classes give Jay an opportunity to fit his system to the needs of the individual student.

"Let's assume I'm a tailor," explains Jay, "You come into my tailor shop, and I ask you to try on a 44 long suit. But the 44 long suit doesn't fit. I'm not going to try to mold you into the physical needs of the suit No! I'm going to alter that suit until it fits you perfectly. And that's just what I have to do with the karate I teach. Everything I do is based on the individual"

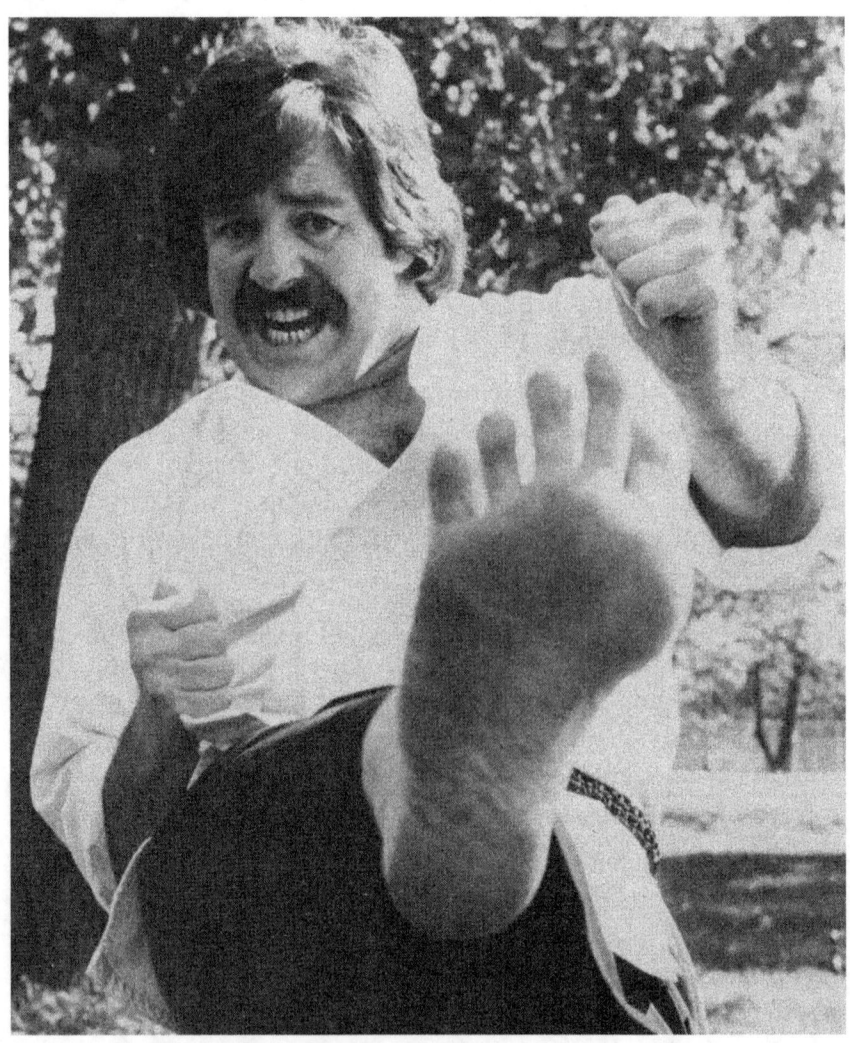

Jay T. Will teaches the Kenpo style of karate. Jay's respect for the individual originally led him into Kenpo. As a martial art, Kenpo is characterized by a flexibility, and an adaptability, which can be found in few others arts.

"Let's take Tae Kwon Do, as an example," suggests Jay. "That art is very oriented toward kicking techniques. Not everybody is physically capable of kicking well. But few Tae Kwon Do instructors make allowance for that. If you study Tae Kwon Do, you are going to learn to kick. And if you can't kick, they're not going to teach you how to punch."

"In other words, you do it the way they do it, or you don't do it at all. They make you fit the style, but in Kenpo, the way I teach it, the style fits you. If you're a good kicker, we'll build a fighting system which emphasizes that. If you're a good puncher, we'll emphasize that your strong points are perfected, and your weak points are improved. That's Kenpo."

Kenpo can be regarded rightfully as the first American martial art. This art grew up in Hawaii, Professor William K. S. Chow combined the soft elements of kung-fu, which he learned from his father, with the hard elements of karate, which he learned from James Mitose, a Japanese-American preacher. Thus, like the culture it sprang from, modem Kenpo contains many contrasting elements.

"If you look at five different Kenpo instructors," says Jay, "they'll all be doing different things. I don't mean different techniques, just that things are visibly different. For instance, a small and fast instructor might do a lot of those little, flashy moves. But for me, since I'm big and physical, I'll just grab and punch the opponent's brains out."

"I like Kenpo because it offers the instructor so much variety in developing his students. There are punching techniques and there are kicking techniques, There are fast techniques and there are power techniques. Like the Chinese systems, Kenpo uses a lot of circular and inward movements. Then, too, there are direct straight-line movements like in the hard styles, such as Shotokan Karate. Kenpo combines the best of all worlds."

The Kenpo system was refined well beyond Professor Chow's original concept by Ed Parker. Ed Parker is the most revered instructor in the history of American karate. Parker examined Professor Chow's Kenpo with the eyes of a boxer, and the experience of a street fighter. He introduced concepts and principles, still not practiced by other systems.

Parker viewed his fighting art as an alphabet of motion. The more letters you have in your alphabet, the more words you can create. And the more words you create, the more sentences you can write. And the more sentences you write, the more paragraphs you can record. And so on.

The alphabet analogy is Ed Parker's poetic explanation of the very practical principle of duplicity. On offense, a Kenpo practitioner does not merely strike, then move away. But rather, whenever possible, he will continue the attack with devastating follow-up techniques. The more techniques you have in your alphabet of motion, the more flexible you become in your ability to pursue the opponent.

On defense, the Kenpo practitioner prefers to redirect, or parry, an attack rather than meet brute force head on with a block. After an opponent's attack has been redirected, the Kenpo practitioner will counterattack, again using the principle of duplicity.

The principle of duplicity will continue to apply until the opponent has been subdued, knocked out, or taken to the ground. Flexibility remains the keynote of Kenpo even to the end. There is no fixed pattern for the conclusion of a fight.

Jay T. Will learned his Kenpo directly from the master, Ed Parker, and always consistent with Parker's philosophy of flexibility, Will has continued to grow, and add new letters to his Kenpo alphabet. He is a physically awesome man who expresses himself best through physical contact It is not surprising that he would seek his technical growth in the arena.

Before he left tournament competition in 1972. Will had won, at one time or another, almost all major tournaments from coast to coast. Also, during that time, he became close friends with heavyweight

karate king Joe Lewis, and trained with him often. Jay T Will was the country's leading full-contact referee, and one of the most sought-after point-count officials.

All of these elements have influenced Jay's no non-sense approach to instruction. "I think it's very hard for any guy to teach how to fight when he has never fought. In fact, I think it's virtually impossible. Not that he has to be a champion, but ... Look at football. 1 can't think of one football coach with any kind of success rate in pro or college football who wasn't at least a one-time player. I'm not saying they were all "Heisman Trophy" winners, or even All- Americans but, hell, they got to play the game."

"The only way a man can teach you well is if he knows that the techniques will work. Now, how is he going to know his techniques work if he's never done the damn things?"

"I don't believe any karate instructor, including myself, has used all his self-defense techniques in a street situation, because it's not true. Competition, particularly full-contact karate competition, is about as close as you're going to come. That's how you'll find out what works, and what doesn't."

Without practical experience, Jay insists, you will teach techniques that work in theory, but not in reality. "I once studied this Chinese style. And they had this front kick which was great in theory. The leg was hardly cocked, then the little devil snuck right in on an op- ponent. You can't see it coming, and it hits really fast. But that technique doesn't work at all in the street. It doesn't have enough power to intimidate an opponent, so he'll just charge right through it."

The techniques Jay teaches, on the other hand, have been tried and proven. In tournament competition, Jay stresses the value of explosive movements, and cutting the circle. But for self-defense, he teaches the value of flexibility. In the book, "Advanced Kenpo", all of the techniques demonstrated are at once practical, and powerful. But the defender must always be ready to adapt the techniques to the situation.

"It's like when the guy pulled the gun on me. You don't have time to think. You simply adapt to the situation, and react. For me, my defense was to walk back into the studio. That wasn't a situation to fight it out. Karate and bullets don't mix."

ABOUT THE AUTHOR

Jay T. Will began studying Kenpo karate in Santa Monica, California, in 1966. He found it a stimulating, competitive and disciplined sport that appealed to his penchant for physical contact.

Will's national fame as a tournament champion came in the Midwest, America's heartland. His grand championships include: Ohio State Championships, National Kenpo Karate Championships, East/West All-Star Tourney, Ohio/Pennsylvania Tournament of Champions, Pro-Am Karate Championships and Pennsylvania Tournament of Champions.

Retired from competition, Will stays active as the country's leading full-contact referee. He flies across the U.S., and to Europe, to fulfill his officiating duties. More recently, he has become involved in television and movies, appearing on "Battlestar Galactica," "Eisheid," "Jaguar Lives" and "Meteor."

www.ingramcontent.com/pod-product-compliance
Lightning Source LLC
Chambersburg PA
CBHW080737230426
43665CB00020B/2776